CAMBRIDGE LIBRARY COLLECTION

Books of enduring scholarly value

Travel and Exploration

The history of travel writing dates back to the Bible, Caesar, the Vikings and the Crusaders, and its many themes include war, trade, science and recreation. Explorers from Columbus to Cook charted lands not previously visited by Western travellers, and were followed by merchants, missionaries, and colonists, who wrote accounts of their experiences. The development of steam power in the nineteenth century provided opportunities for increasing numbers of 'ordinary' people to travel further, more economically, and more safely, and resulted in great enthusiasm for travel writing among the reading public. Works included in this series range from first-hand descriptions of previously unrecorded places, to literary accounts of the strange habits of foreigners, to examples of the burgeoning numbers of guidebooks produced to satisfy the needs of a new kind of traveller - the tourist.

Our Journey to Sinai

First published in 1896, this work by Agnes Bensly (d. 1900), wife of the Orientalist and biblical scholar Robert Bensly (1831–93), describes the journey undertaken by a party of scholars to St Catherine's Monastery on Mount Sinai in 1893. In the previous year, sisters Agnes Smith Lewis and Margaret Dunlop Gibson had discovered the Sinai Palimpsest, the earliest-known Syriac version of the Gospels. The purpose of the Benslys' mission was to aid them in transcribing and deciphering the Palimpsest. Beginning with the party's arrival in Cairo, the book describes the preparation for the trip, their journey across the desert, and life in the monastery. However, relations between the members of the party deteriorated; Gibson and Lewis wrote their own accounts of the expedition (also available in this series), and Mrs Bensly's narrative is defensive of the role of her husband, who died days after their return to England.

T0352095

Cambridge University Press has long been a pioneer in the reissuing of out-of-print titles from its own backlist, producing digital reprints of books that are still sought after by scholars and students but could not be reprinted economically using traditional technology. The Cambridge Library Collection extends this activity to a wider range of books which are still of importance to researchers and professionals, either for the source material they contain, or as landmarks in the history of their academic discipline.

Drawing from the world-renowned collections in the Cambridge University Library, and guided by the advice of experts in each subject area, Cambridge University Press is using state-of-the-art scanning machines in its own Printing House to capture the content of each book selected for inclusion. The files are processed to give a consistently clear, crisp image, and the books finished to the high quality standard for which the Press is recognised around the world. The latest print-on-demand technology ensures that the books will remain available indefinitely, and that orders for single or multiple copies can quickly be supplied.

The Cambridge Library Collection brings back to life books of enduring scholarly value (including out-of-copyright works originally issued by other publishers) across a wide range of disciplines in the humanities and social sciences and in science and technology.

Our Journey to Sinai

A Visit to the Convent of St. Catarina

AGNES BENSLY

CAMBRIDGE
UNIVERSITY PRESS

CAMBRIDGE UNIVERSITY PRESS

Cambridge, New York, Melbourne, Madrid, Cape Town,
Singapore, São Paolo, Delhi, Tokyo, Mexico City

Published in the United States of America by Cambridge University Press, New York

www.cambridge.org
Information on this title: www.cambridge.org/9781108043373

© in this compilation Cambridge University Press 2012

This edition first published 1896
This digitally printed version 2012

ISBN 978-1-108-04337-3 Paperback

CONVENT OF ST. CATARINA ON MOUNT SINAI, FROM BELOW.

OUR JOURNEY TO SINAI

*A VISIT TO THE CONVENT OF
ST. CATARINA*

BY

MRS. R. L. BENSLY

WITH A CHAPTER ON THE SINAI PALIMPSEST

ILLUSTRATED FROM PHOTOGRAPHS TAKEN BY THE AUTHOR

THE RELIGIOUS TRACT SOCIETY

56 PATERNOSTER ROW AND 65 ST. PAUL'S CHURCHYARD

1896

OXFORD
HORACE HART, PRINTER TO THE UNIVERSITY

EDITOR'S PREFACE

THIS little book was first written in Braille type (for the use of the blind) by Mrs. Bensly, whose eyesight failed soon after her husband's death, which occurred three days after his return to Cambridge. It is now transcribed and printed at the desire of her children and friends. Mr. F. C. Burkitt, M.A., has added greatly to the value of the book by allowing part of the account which he gave of the Sinai Palimpsest at the Church Congress in October, 1895, to appear as Chapter VIII.

Although the book necessarily travels over part of the ground covered by *How the Codex was Found*, it is believed that a much wider circle than the purely personal one for which the account was first written will welcome this sketch, and the side-lights it throws upon one of the most important Biblical discoveries of modern times.

CONTENTS

LIST OF ILLUSTRATIONS

—◆—

NEAR AYIN MUSA.

INTRODUCTION

WE were quite young, only just married, when we first planned to visit the lands of the Bible together. We read the accounts of Eastern travellers, we bought maps and guide-books, we saluted each other with Bedouin phrases and gestures. My husband had been for some time an eager student of Oriental customs and languages; thirty years later he had become one of the first scholars in Europe; yet that early desire had not been fulfilled. The education of our children, stress of work, lack of money, the many changes and chances of this mortal life, had kept us at home.   In the spring of 1892 Mrs. Lewis and Mrs. Gibson, two Scottish ladies, known as great travellers, brought from the Convent of St. Catarina on Mount Sinai wonderful accounts and photographs of early Biblical MSS., especially of a Syriac palimpsest of most venerable appearance.

In olden times, before the invention of paper-mill and printing-press, most books were written on parchment, a preparation of goat- or sheep-skin.   This being expensive and not always easy to get, industrious writers were sometimes driven to use what we might now be inclined to call ' waste paper ' ; they took an old book, which they did not care to read any longer, or of which they possessed several copies, they scrubbed and scraped the writing off the leathern leaves, and then proceeded to write their new book on the old pages.   But their predecessors had used very good ink, which would not be entirely effaced, and we can often trace the earlier writing, in faint yellow marks, between the lines, and even between the words and letters of the later work ; such a doubly-filled volume is called a palimpsest.

In the early summer months Professor Bensly's time was fully occupied with University business ; but in the Long Vacation he carefully examined the photographs brought by Mrs. Lewis and Mrs. Gibson, in company with his friend and former pupil, Mr. F. C. Burkitt, of Trinity College.   I sat in the room where the two scholars, with their heads close together, were deciphering some of the under-writing, and I well remember their exclamations of gladness and triumph when they found it to contain the earliest Syriac translation of our Gospels, made in the second century, and known hitherto only from fragments and quotations. Though the Evangelists wrote in Greek, Syriac was the native language of our Lord and His disciples, and whenever the actual words of Christ are quoted : 'ephphatha,' 'talitha cumi,' 'eli, eli, lama sabachthani,' they are not in Greek, but in Syriac (or rather in Aramaic, of which Syriac is a dialect). This early version, then, is invaluable, as giving us more nearly than perhaps any other writing, the very sound of the words which our Lord uttered.

Both Mr. Bensly and Mr. Burkitt saw that it would be impossible to recover more than a few lines here and there from the photographs alone. They at once resolved to go and see the original ; their wives claimed the privilege of accompanying them. The ladies above mentioned volunteered to go a second time, to assist the party with their experience in Eastern travel and with their knowledge of modern Greek, the language of the monks on Sinai ; and the six travellers arranged to start about Christmas, the early part of the year being the most favourable season for crossing the desert. A seventh traveller, a friend of Mrs. Lewis, Mr. Rendel Harris, of Clare College, joined us later on, at Suez. We all felt the importance of the undertaking, we all valued the privilege of assisting, in some way, at the recovery of such a treasure. To my husband and myself, this journey was also the realization of early dreams, the fulfilment of a never quite-forgotten fancy: and now as I sit in darkness and solitude, and remember that wonderful time, so different from the even tenor of our English lives, it seems to recede again into the realms of romance: I think of the boundless freedom of the desert, of its golden light and eternal sunshine; I listen to the sound of falling waters and to the waving of the palm-trees, where I wander hand in hand with my beloved, and I hardly know: Is it a dream of the past? is it a vision of the future?

But now to business; for this book is intended to give a practical account of 'Our Journey to Sinai'; how we bestrode our camels, how we ate and drank and slept in the desert, how we settled in the convent garden, climbed to the top of the holy mountain, and finally carried home, in our saddle-bags, the hard-won transcription of the great palimpsest.

CHAPTER I

CAIRO

AT home it was mid-winter, when we, in warm and sunny weather, arrived at Cairo, at the far-famed Shepheard's Hotel. It was full of travellers from all parts of the world; and many of them made it, like ourselves, a welcome resting-place, before going further south or east, and enjoyed, from its broad terrace, their first full view of Oriental life, by watching the moving panorama of the street below. It was like a scene from the Arabian Nights revived for our benefit, as we reclined in comfortable rocking-chairs under the large awning in front of the hotel, and leisurely sipped our afternoon tea. On the pavement, close to the terrace-wall, squatted a row of porters, each on his own little mat; their legs were bare, but their heads carefully wrapped in bright-coloured turbans. Motionless they sat, the smoke from their pipes was the only sign of life. But the landlord calls, and instantly, with loud vociferations, a dozen brown arms are fighting for the letter in his hand. The conqueror hides it in the bosom of his long blue shirt, his only visible garment, and is lost in the crowd. The others return contentedly to bask in sunshine and tobacco-smoke.

Two handsome fellows, in white tunics with flowing sleeves and gold-embroidered vests, run abreast, at full speed, along the middle of the road: they are the fore-runners of a greatman's carriage. Here it is —a big, burly, moody-faced boy in semi-European attire sits by the side of an elderly mentor. It is the young Khedive: the crowd halts for a moment, and salutes the sovereign by touching brow and breast with the fingers of the right hand. A few devout subjects prostrate themselves, with the face to the ground, as in the mosque when the name of Allah is mentioned. He is gone, returning to his mother's country residence from his daily visit to the official palace in Cairo. Now native soldiers march past, with their band, led by an English officer. Whatever these sons of the desert may think of drill and confinement, evidently they are proud of their smart uniform, and enjoy the martial strains of the music.

A Greek priest in black gown and high cylindrical cap makes his way, with downcast eyes, to cloister or cathedral, seemingly unobserved by the multitude. A dark-skinned policeman, who seems hardly at home in his tight coat and trousers, pats a riotous nigger gently on the back, coaxing him to move on to a more convenient spot. He looks fierce enough to bully any foreign traveller, but cannot speak roughly to his African brother. A wealthy merchant, bound for his place in the bazaar, trots along on a swift-footed white donkey, with trappings of purple velvet. The little black servant-boy runs behind, out of breath, but thinks it his duty to whack the donkey each time he gets near enough to reach it with his stick. Hindoo ayahs, daintily dressed in Indian embroideries, with jewelled rings in nose and underlip, lead their fair nurslings carefully through the crowd.

The native women are covered and veiled, from head to foot, by the yashmak, a long navy-blue cloak; it is fastened, above the nose, by a curious brass ornament, and leaves only the dark eyes and darker eyebrows visible. Some of them have been marketing, and carry large flat baskets with fruit and vegetables on their heads. One of them has her naked little baby sitting astride on her shoulder; it clutches the mother's draperies with its curling toes and sticky little fingers, and sucks composedly a bit of sugar-cane, the usual bon-bon of Egyptian children. Alas, its pretty brown face is besmeared with the sweet juice, and almost covered by flies.

Every kind of commodity is offered for sale in the street, one always in louder and shriller tones than the other. There are the water-carriers, with heavy stone jars on their heads or with water-skins, in the shape of little black pigs, slung across their backs. There are vendors of lemonade with shining tin cans and pannikins, pastrycooks with trays full of bright-coloured sweetmeats, women laden with bananas and

B

oranges, and the Bedouin from the desert, who carry palm-nuts and dates in the capacious sleeves of their bournous. These appeal chiefly to the natives ; while brass trays and Persian rugs, ostrich feathers and bamboo canes, basket-work and pottery from the Soudan, relics from the ancient tombs, and roses fresh-gathered from the sultana's gardens are cried and held before the face of every man or woman in modern attire.

The most noisy and numerous of all the people in the road are the donkey-boys and the beggars. Every donkey-boy is, of course, accompanied by his donkey. These African animals differ much from their English brethren. Taller and stronger, with neatly shaped heads and docile manners, they are generally well fed and groomed, at least in Cairo, where everybody seems to ride them, and where they are largely kept for the benefit of the tourists. Their owners, bright little urchins in cotton shirts and white skull-caps, introduce them to every decently dressed foot-passenger, each of them as 'the quickest and cleverest donkey in Cairo,' and vary their names from the native Ali or Omar to Bismarck, Napoleon, or Grand Old Man, according to the nationality of the coveted customer. The beggars, old or young, blind or sighted, crippled or able-bodied, half naked or jealously hidden under the dirtiest of blankets and rags, never cease from stretching forth their hands and from uttering their cry of ' Baksheesh.' They squat in every sunny corner, and besiege every stranger whom they can reasonably suppose to carry loose piastres in his pocket.

It is wonderful to see how the Arab drivers steer their light open carriages safely through this living stream. Indeed, they increase the general din by the shrillest of warnings; but the very frequency of their shouts tends to make them unheeded. In this motley crowd the residents and visitors from Western Europe would look incongruous in their sombre attire, had they not already somewhat conformed to the Oriental taste for brightness and colour by wearing Syrian sashes, and by tying gaily striped or snow-white kufeejahs around their hats. Moreover, all Government officials, from the Khedive down to the lowest clerk, wear indoors and out of doors the red fez, or Turkish cap, ornamented by a long blue tassel, whether their other garments are Egyptian or European. There are many such hybrid costumes (black coats and red caps), for this neighbourhood of Shepheard's Hotel is, after all, but modern Cairo. The street is wide, well-paved and drained, the houses are built in French fashion, and the shops managed like those of Paris or London. Old Cairo, the city of the caliphs, must be sought in the native quarter, in its coffee-houses, mosques, and bazaars.

Often, during the following weeks, did we wander down the Mooskee or Mûskî, the chief commercial road of the old town, escorted each time by a number of importunate boys, genuine little street arabs, who wanted us to ride on their donkeys, offered to show us the way, and poured no end of information into our ears. We preferred to go on foot, we required no guide, we understood little of their language, and we gave them no baksheesh, yet we never got quite rid of their clamour and their company. The street was narrow, the pavement execrable, and cleanliness an unknown luxury; yet we easily forgot these drawbacks under the magic influence of the *lux ex Oriente* that illumined all our surroundings. The upper stories project from both sides of the way, so that only a slender strip of dark blue sky is visible above. The old Moorish doorways are more or less richly ornamented by carved scrolls and painted texts from the Koran, the windows are few and far between, and all covered by screens or blinds of curiously carved fretwork, admitting air and light, but guarding the fair inmates from every inquisitive eye. The chief rooms all open towards inner courts and galleries; and now and then, when one of the heavy doors opened to admit a water-carrier or a silk-merchant, we caught glimpses of cool greenery and sparkling fountains within. The ladies are seldom seen in the street, closely veiled and jealously guarded, but the men seem to transact all their business out-of-doors. We watched a scribe, who had established himself with his carpet and writing-tablet in a quiet corner. His ink-horn was safely stuck in his belt, as he listened to the whispers of two veiled females, who leant over his shoulders and looked with amazement at the mystic signs of the reed-pen that were to convey their messages of love or jealousy to some distant friend. Further on, in a little square, an eager crowd had collected round a native conjurer. Without any of the tools and trappings seen at a modern juggler's performances, he sat down on a piece of matting in full daylight, and began by producing young chickens from his mouth, and serpents from his ears ; the creatures he manipulated and changed and multiplied in a most bewildering manner, and I do not know who admired him most, the Arabs, who believed him to be a great magician inspired by Allah, or we, who had never seen such skill and cleverness as he displayed in these inexplicable tricks. Close to him, in front of a barber's shop, hair-cutting and shaving were going on in public : and here we saw for the first time the bare head of a true Muhammedan, almost clean shaven, but with a long tuft of hair at the back. The coffee shops, all open and overflowing into the roadway, were always full of loungers, who reclined on carpets and cushions, and enjoyed the mixed flavour of tobacco and coffee. Some five or six of them would sit in a circle on the ground and play a kind of dominoes, or else listen spell-bound to one of their professional story-tellers. Our children were never more charmed with their nursery tales than these grave, black-bearded men with the fables and legends that are thus related to them.

In this same street are several small mosques, frequented chiefly by the lower classes. Their slender minarets and more imposing doorways distinguish the otherwise bare walls from the surrounding houses. These minarets are not unlike our lighthouses in shape. They are crowned at the top by a little cupola and a round gallery, from which the muezzins (who in England would be called church clerks) call the faithful to prayer at fixed hours throughout the day. We had heard and read so much about these calls to prayer that we were disappointed how little notice they attracted among the people. Now and then we saw a true believer, who prostrated himself and recited his prayers at the precise time of noon or sunset, whether in the open desert or in the crowded city; but this was an exception from the general rule. It may be that the winter, when Cairo is flooded by strangers, is not the most favourable season for the display of native piety—at least one of the boys tried to explain this in his broken English : ' Now very much stranger, very much donkey wanted, no time for prayer; in summer, no work, no baksheesh, very much prayer, very much mosque.' Yet even now we never found a mosque quite empty. ' Put off thy shoes from off thy feet, for the place whereon thou standest is holy ground.' The prayer-carpet, that covers the greater part of the floor in every mosque, represents this holy ground to the Muhammedans. In the alabaster mosque of the Khedive, and in other wealthy places, it consists of the best and costliest fabrics, but in poorer quarters it is of matting only, and sometimes sadly dilapidated ; but no dusty shoe nor travel-stained foot is allowed to touch it. Before entering, all worshippers take off their shoes, and wash hands and feet in the nearest fountain. Most mosques have one of their own in a shady court or just inside the gate. Some of the men carry a towel in their sleeve, others come forward and kneel down with bright drops glistening on their bronze-coloured limbs. They repeat their prayers in a rhythmical kind of undertone, swinging the body gently to and fro, as if to keep time with the voice, and touching the ground at intervals with the palms of their hands and their forehead. They look neither to the right nor to the left, and go out as quietly as they came in. There seemed to be no special time or form of service, but we generally heard overhead the measured tones of a reader who recited parts of the Koran.

A few years ago all visitors had to take off their shoes at the entrance ; there is now an innovation in the shape of large straw slippers, which an attendant tied over our boots. We were then allowed to enter, but it was a clumsy contrivance ; the knotted strings would get undone, and we had to stand on one leg until the slipper was readjusted. Not a reverential proceeding, but it may have saved us from a cold in the head. Though all pictures, even representations of flowers and foliage, are strictly forbidden, the fashionable mosques are most beautifully decorated. The quaint shapes of the Arabic letters lend themselves easily to graceful patterns for scrolls and panels ;

and texts from the Koran, in mosaic of gold and precious stones, cover great part of the walls, while coloured marbles, silken hangings, and hundreds of silver lamps complete the rest. But here we found the interiors somewhat dark and desolate. The kibla, or prayer-niche, in the direction of Mekka, towards which the worshippers bow, is a plain door-shaped recess in the wall : there is also a kind of balcony for the reader, a screened gallery for the women, and sometimes the tomb of the saint or benefactor that gives his name to the place (a cubicle of stone with a low entrance, covered inside and outside with tinselled pieces of cloth)

Yet there can be no greater contrast than between the cool quietude of these little mosques and the noisy excitement of the neighbouring bazaars. An incredible amount of merchandise is here heaped up in a comparatively small space, for these bazaars are not, as one might suppose, wide market-places, but very narrow lanes, that cross and meet and intersect each other in every possible angle and direction, forming a labyrinth in which we lost ourselves for hours together, returning repeatedly, without knowing it, to the same spot, but finding there always new objects of interest. Each lane is devoted to a par-ticular branch of industry or commerce : there is a silk bazaar, a brass bazaar, a carpet bazaar, and so on. The overhanging houses nearly meet at the top, where strips of carpet, tent-cloths, and palm-branches are stretched from roof to roof to keep out the sun.

In England such a contrivance would leave the traders in darkness; but under the bright sky of Egypt, where clouds are almost unknown, light is abundant. The lower parts of the houses form a continuous row of small open shops, apparently without front walls. They are separated from the roadway only by a threshold covered by cushions and carpets; here the merchant reclines, and here the customer sits down by his side. Sometimes we found the former engaged in reading the Koran. If so, he would quietly finish his verse or his chapter before betaking himself to business. But these Arabs are born traders, and know how to get a good bargain out of the unwary traveller. One wants more time and experience than we possessed to buy anything at its true value. They always began by asking three or four times the legitimate price. We answered by offering somewhat less than we intended to give, and a long discussion then followed, which ended in meeting half-way, and in our paying at least double what we ought to have spent. When one of the dealers had imposed on us more than his elastic conscience would allow, he graciously offered us a little present—an embroidered mat or a flagon with a drop of rose-oil. I possess several of these keepsakes, which remind me of pleasant hours spent in the bazaars, but also of the facility with which we were gulled.

Within this network of narrow passages and blind alleys are also, here and there, larger courts and

halls secluded by high walls from the turmoil without, with richly carved gateways, balconies, and
fountains, probably the remains of ancient mosques
and palaces. These are now used as warehouses by
the wealthier merchants. We visited one of them
several times: he was a dealer in carpets, a fine old
man in a long kaftan of purple silk trimmed with
fur and costly embroidery. His place had once
formed part of a mosque; the women's gallery was
now occupied by his clerks and accountants, and
the beautiful Moorish arches and the dark walls
above were covered with the richest of Oriental
hangings and rugs; heavy rolls of the same fabrics
were ranged all around, forming luxurious divans,
where we sat by his side, conversing amicably as
well as people can do who understood little or
nothing of each other's language, about the weather,
the influx of strangers, and the rising of the Nile.
An attendant in spotless white brought coffee in
little cups of most delicate china, and the host
handed us an ivory box of sweets. Nothing was
said of buying or selling, but his servants unrolled
carpet after carpet before our eyes and spread them
at our feet until the floor of the vast apartment was
covered with a two- or three-fold layer of the softest
colours and textures. Once or twice we timidly
asked the price of a specially bewitching prayer-carpet.
It was too high; we could not hope to bring it, by
the longest discussion, within the limits of our purse.
But though we came again and again to admire

and not to buy, we were always received with the same dignified courtesy. From sunrise to sunset those bazaars are full of buyers and sightseers, of natives and foreigners, of men, women, and donkeys, shouting and braying and pushing three abreast through passages where there seems hardly room for one ; but at nightfall the crowds disappear, gaily caparisoned donkeys take the owners home to their harem, busy servants put up folding-doors and shutters, and the poor watchmen lie down on the pavement outside their master's door. Here they spend the night, simply wrapped in blankets, looking like bundles of old clothes, or ensconced in narrow coffin-shaped baskets. No doubt they sleep soundly, but only across their bodies could an entrance be effected.

Here below the native element still reigns undisturbed, but the old Citadel above is entirely in the hands of the English. From the last steep spur of the Mokattam hills it dominates the town, and affords at the same time a beautiful view over the surrounding country. At the foot of the hill stands the old mosque of Sultan Hassan, the stateliest mosque in all Egypt, but now forsaken and left to decay in honour of its modern successor on the summit— inferior in every way except in its clothing of gold and alabaster. We drove up by the wide carriage road that is now preferred to the narrow passage between high walls (formerly the only available approach) where the unhappy Mamelouks were surprised

as in a trap, and massacred to the last man by order
of Mehemet Ali, when returning from a banquet in
the Citadel. The tall figures and fair faces of the
English sentinels who now stood at the gates and
took our cards were pleasant to behold, and the
quiet demeanour of the soldiers who loitered on the
newly washed pavement of the parade-ground, in
their cool undress, fell in agreeably with the fresh
breezes from the west after the heat and dust of the
streets below. There, at our feet, lay the vast city,
its yellow-gray walls (sandstone from the Mokattam
hills) unstained by smoke or damp, spread out like
a map, with its flat roofs and innumerable minarets,
with its palaces and gardens; and beyond it the
fruitful valley of Egypt and the sacred river Nile
winding away into the distance, with its white-
winged sailing-boats, looking from afar like so many
sea-gulls skimming the waves. A low range of hills
bounded the view towards the east, but the sands
of the desert gleamed on the western horizon; and
there, dark and sharply defined against the golden
sunset sky, rose the familiar shapes of the Pyramids,
so familiar from nursery books and Bible pictures,
from drawings and paintings of every kind! We
could hardly believe that this was not another picture
but reality itself; it fascinated our eyes: again and
again we turned to those wonders of the world; we
gazed until the shades of evening fell and the gates
of the Citadel had to be closed.

We felt that we could not leave Egypt without

having seen the Pyramids face to face. So, very early one morning, my husband and myself took our places on the top of the coach that plied daily between Cairo and Ghizeh (a distance of twelve or fourteen miles). Four quick horses took us quickly through the busy streets to the long bridge over the Nile. It is flanked at both ends by large gates, with heavy stone lions on the head of the piers. These gates are shut for two hours about noon, when the incessant traffic from shore to shore slackens a little during the heat of the day, and the bridge itself is then opened for the sake of the shipping. The ancient river was at its best; not overflowing all the low-lying lands, as in August and September, nor leaving its sandbanks and shallows bare, as in March and April, but a broad powerful stream, reflecting the palaces and gardens on its bank, and alive with steamers, sailing and rowing boats, of every possible build and destination. Just above the bridge some of Cook's floating hotels, that take every winter thousands of visitors up to the cataracts, were flying their pennons. On the opposite side the graceful dahabeeyahs (private house-boats) were ranged along the shore, waiting for the north-wind to take them up to Luxor and Philae for their sunny holiday on the blue waters. We had already boarded several of them, whose owners we knew, and had admired the taste and ingenuity that make these temporary homes so cosy and comfort-able; the upper decks especially, with their awnings and carpets, with their bamboo lounges and tropical flower-stands, form the most attractive of drawing-rooms. They differ much in size and style, from the white and gold summer-palace of the Khedive to the snug little boat belonging to the American Mission; but they are all alike in shape, long and slender, with high slanting yards and huge three-cornered sails; and they carry invariably, at the stern, their own provision-boat, with a large hen-coop full of fowls and one solitary sheep. Down the middle of the stream float lazily the native market boats, clumsy-looking, almost square, and heavily laden with cattle and corn, or piled half-way up the mast with fruit and vegetables. Larger cargo-boats take foreign merchandise up, and bring down the sugar from the huge manufactories on the Upper Nile. The swift little mail-steamers, with the half-moon flying at the mast-head, provide for the postal and passenger traffic throughout the length of the land; and innumerable neat sailing and rowing boats flit up and down, and from shore to shore; the sailors lie lazily smoking on the sunny deck, and the rowers time their work to a low monotonous chant. In a village near the further end of the bridge a kind of fair was going on, and for the next half-hour, as we drove along the high embankment by the side of the river, we met a continuous stream of market-people, with strings of camels and donkeys, carrying their country produce to the capital.

We met picturesque family groups : father, mother, and children on the same camel, together with a live sheep and sundry fowls, held lovingly in the children's arms ; other parties went on foot, urging on their poor, overburdened donkey, while some had to carry their bundles and baskets themselves, when the heaviest load would always be laid on the head of the woman. We passed the entrance to the princely gardens of Ghizeh. The palace, with its lofty halls and galleries, is now the museum for the treasures of ancient Egypt. Here, after 4,000 years' rest in their rocky graves, are deposited, in glass cases, the mummies of the Pharaohs and the golden ornaments of Queen Hatasu. Here the walls are all covered with bas-reliefs and inscriptions, taken from temples and tombs, and revealing to us their religion and history ; and here, among flowering shrubs, is the grave of the great explorer Mariette, guarded by four of his favourite sphinxes.

Soon after passing the palace gates we left the river and entered the beautiful avenue of lebbek trees (thornless acacias) that leads in a straight line from the Nile to the Pyramids. On both sides lay fruitful fields of corn and clover, villages and farmsteads, surrounded, almost hidden, by high eucalyptus trees ; herds of kine and buffaloes stood more than knee-deep in the rich pastures, and droves of camels, unattended, crossed our road. The canals were still full from the last inundation, and water-wheels were at work on all sides to fill the rivulets that intersect the fields in every direction. The road was in excellent order and the ride altogether delightful, but its

interest centred in the view of the Pyramids ahead.
Hidden now and then by intervening trees, they seemed
to have gained in size each time they re-appeared,
until the coach drew up at the foot of the natural
platform on which these giant mausoleums rise.

At the very edge of the desert lies a little plateau,
about a mile square, and nowhere higher than 100 ft.
This was the burial ground of the great 6,000 years
ago. Here stood seven or eight pyramids and several
other sanctuaries, while the ground itself was honey-
combed by temples and tomb-chambers cut in the
solid rock. They wore used as quarries by the Turks
in building the mosques and palaces of Cairo, or
overwhelmed and filled up by the shifting sands of
the desert. But the two largest pyramids have braved
storms and depredations, and from a little distance
look almost intact, though their outer covering of
polished stone is gone except a little piece at the very
top, and innumerable huge blocks have been torn away
from around the base, some of them still strewing
the ground, half buried in rubbish and sand. The
impression of power which the Pyramids make upon
the beholder must not be measured by their height
alone—which is, after all, not much greater than that
of the cathedrals of Strasburg and Cologne—the area
which they cover, and the massiveness of their construction, must be considered. We rested and lunched
in the shadow of the Pyramid of Cheops, and we were
almost painfully oppressed by its grandeur.

But more surprising still than the size of the Pyra-

mids, was to us that of the Great Sphinx, which lies
a few hundred yards to the south, now almost entirely
freed from its covering of sand. It once held a temple
between its gigantic paws, and some of the votive
inscriptions can still be read on the ruins below.
Seen close at hand, the head of the sphinx is little
more than an unshapen mass of rock; but we watched
it from afar in the quiet evening light, until we saw
dawning in the marred and battered features their
ancient expression of awful solemnity. The walls of
the newly excavated tombs are covered with bas-
reliefs and inscriptions as sharp and clear as if fresh
from the chisel: but the sarcophagi, the images of the
gods, and the sacrificial tables are now preserved in
the museum at Ghizeh. We took tea with a friend,
who was staying at Mena-House, the beautiful hotel
at the foot of the Pyramids, and the coachman's horn
sounded all too soon. My only outward memorial of
this day is a small photograph, taken by the same
kind friend. It represents the learned professor and
his homely wife, with the awful background of Pyramid
and Sphinx. We stayed three weeks at Cairo, not
half long enough to see, much less to learn, all it has
to show and to teach; but we were only pilgrims passing through, and would not have delayed so long, had
not the necessary preparations for our ride across the
desert kept us back from day to day.

CHAPTER II

PREPARATIONS

OUR first business, after arriving in Cairo, was to look for a trustworthy dragoman (interpreter and guide). We were soon besieged by applicants: without special letters of introduction they were not allowed to enter the hotel itself; but no sooner did we come out on to the terrace than they got hold of us. If we sat down, they took the next chair; if we went out, they walked by our side along the road. They brought from out their sleeves a formidable array of testimonials, spread them on the nearest table, or—if more convenient—on the pavement at our feet, and would not let us go until we had perused the very last of them. They were, most of them, natives of Cairo, robust middle-aged men with dark intelligent features, and a moderate knowledge of English. They were clad alike in the usual garb of well-to-do Egyptians: a full skirt of dark cloth reaching below the knees, a short open coat or jacket of similar material, and a waistcoat of silk or velvet with rich embroideries in silver and gold; they all wore soft Indian shawls carefully arranged as belt and as turban ; their names did not vary very much ; Ahmed and Muhammed, Musa (Moses), and Ibrahim occurring again and again in different combinations ; and even their testimonials had a kind of family likeness, setting forth in general terms the owner's honesty, intelligence, and amiable disposition. Now and then we found the signature of a famous traveller or a well-known resident of Cairo ; but we had been warned not to trust overmuch to these papers, as the real owner of a valuable certificate is apt to let it out on hire to his less fortunate brethren.

Under these circumstances it was difficult for us to keep the names and persons, and still more so the special virtues and qualifications of our many candidates distinct from each other. Two or three of them, indeed, stood out in high relief from the general company : one, a tall powerful man, over six feet high and more than proportionately broad, tried to commend himself by stroking his ample stomach, and assuring us that he liked to live well himself, and would take care his travellers did the same. But he would not come to terms, and only repeated again and again, ' that Englishmen did not care how much they paid as long as their table was well provided.' Another applicant was a slim youth, a pupil from the American Mission Schools; we found, on questioning him, that he had not been to Sinai, that he did not understand the dialect of the Bedouins, and that he had no experience in camel-riding, but he answered all our objections by exclaiming, with the fervour of a new David :

' I am young and inexperienced, but I am a Christian, and I trust in the good Lord, who will lead us safely across the desert ! ' We could but assure him that we also relied on the blessing of God, and hoped it would not be averted by a more capable dragoman.

At length, after many inquiries and much deliberation, we engaged as our dragoman one Ahmed abd-er-Raheem (the servant of the Most Merciful). He was a strict Muhammedan, yet we took him, chiefly on the warm recommendations of Dr. Watson, the well-known head of the American Mission in Cairo ; and I may here state, once for all, that he gave general satisfaction throughout the journey, and fully justified the good opinion of his patron. Ahmed himself was an ardent admirer of Dr. and Mrs. Watson, and of their lamented predecessor, Dr. Lancing, in whose house he had once been a servant.

Through the kindness of Dr. and Mrs. Watson we were enabled to attend several mission services, both in Arabic and English, and to learn something about their work in the land of Egypt. It lies chiefly among the Kopts, the descendants of the ancient inhabitants, who are still Christians in name, though a blue cross, tattooed on the forearm, is often to them the only witness of Christianity. There are now stations at regular intervals along the Nile, up to the cataracts, with Christian schools and meeting-houses ; and their little dahabeeyah, with one of the super-intendents on board, is always afloat, visiting the outlying flocks and keeping up their connexion with the headquarters in Cairo. But the mission addresses itself also to Muhammedans, and, chiefly by appealing to their love and veneration for Allah it has led many of them into the more excellent way. Aḥmed himself showed no signs of becoming a Christian, but I feel sure that his deep-seated piety, and his strict sense of duty, have been fostered and ennobled by his constant contact with Christianity in its highest form at the home of the American missionaries in Cairo.

Having secured a dragoman, our next step was to draw up a formal contract with him, to be signed and sealed before the English Consul, and again in presence of the Greek Archbishop of Sinai, who resides in Cairo ; he is, by a very old statute, in one person the metropolitan and the abbot of the monastery on Sinai, and, in virtue of that office, a kind of liege-lord over the Towara tribe, through whose territory we would have to pass. When the Emperor Justinian endowed the monastery with worldly goods he also assigned to it, as serfs, some of the surrounding tribes ; and there still exists a nominal subjection, though enforced by no temporal power, according to which the men of the Towara bring their difficulties with other tribes, their differences among themselves, and even their quarrels with their wives, before the monks on Sinai, and never fail to seek their assistance in times of sickness or scarcity.

It was important that Mr. Bensly and Mr. Burkitt should be free to devote all their time and energy to literary work, unencumbered by cares for daily

bread and (worse in this case) for daily water. Aḥmed
had great experience in desert travelling, having
accompanied the English army to Tel-el-Kebir, and
provided for the officers' mess on the very day of
the battle. And so we decided on paying him one
inclusive sum, empowering him to treat in our name

AḤMED.

with monks and Bedouin, to provide tents and tent-
furniture, to secure a proper supply of water, and to
buy food, sufficient not only for the double journey,
but also for a month's sojourn on Sinai, as we could
not reckon on getting anything in the mountains,
beyond, perhaps, a sheep from a passing flock, or

a few vegetables from the gardens of the convent. Half of the money was handed to him at once, the other half was, in his presence, deposited at the bank, to be drawn by him on completion of his work. He was moreover commissioned to give baksheesh, in our name, not to all who asked for it (which would have demanded a purse of inordinate length), but to all whose goodwill it was expedient to secure; and by this latter arrangement we escaped an immense amount of fraud and molestation.

As soon as the contract was signed before the consul, our dragoman began his work: he was now freely admitted into the hotel, and visited us at all hours of the day. For though we had left the arrangements of the caravan entirely in his hands, he was anxious to indulge individual tastes, and came to consult us on every detail. He also, at once, constituted himself our guide, and accompanied us on donkey-back as we drove to the archbishop's palace. Here we were received, at the outer gate, by a porter in ecclesiastical attire, who handed us at the next entrance to a higher official, and so on, from door to door, until a great dignitary of the Church ushered us into the presence of the metropolitan himself, who was seated on a kind of throne in the grandest of episcopal robes. But he did not seem, personally, to feel oppressed by his sanctity. We found a jovial, easy-tempered man, who shook hands with us, treated us to coffee and sweets, and at once ordered his secretary to prepare our letters of introduction to his vice-gerent in the convent on Mount Sinai. We conversed with him by interpreter, and my husband tried to draw his attention to a little book which he had brought with him from England [1]. But his eminence did not care much for new discoveries : ' Four Gospels quite enough for me,' he said, with a deprecatory wave of the hand ; but he nevertheless claimed the neatly bound volume, which had been laid on his table, as a present, causing thereby no little inconvenience to Professor Bensly, who found it difficult to procure another copy in Cairo. Before leaving the precincts, we were introduced to a sheikh of the Towara, who, with his camels and his men, was to escort us across the desert, and had been summoned hither from his tents beyond Suez, to pledge his faith for our safety. He was a picturesque old man, unkempt and unshaven, in the coarsest of garbs, yet with an unspeakable dignity of manner and mien. His outer garment was a kind of inverted sack, of dark brown canvas, with three openings for the head and the arms, and on his feet he had only rough wooden sandals tied with knotted camel-hair string, but a voluminous red and yellow turban seemed to make up for other deficiencies.

On the following day, in a quiet street, behind the hotel, Aḥmed gave us our first lesson in camel-riding, or rather in mounting and dismounting, which is the

---

[1] *The Gospel of St. Peter*, which had only lately been edited from a papyrus found in a tomb near Cairo, and which excited, at the time, much attention in the West.

only awkward part of it. My animal was lying
quietly enough while I got into the saddle, but then
suddenly it rose on its hind legs, with its front knees
still bent on the ground ; I should have been pitched
over its head on to the pavement, if Aḥmed had not
held me ; and it took several days before I got used
to these jerky movements and could keep my seat
without assistance, when the camel was getting up or
lying down again.

We also tried another way of locomotion (in a
covered litter, the usual conveyance of Egyptian
ladies before the introduction of closed carriages).
This time our parade-ground was a sandy track, near
the Tombs of the Caliphs, just outside the city walls.
Here we sat on the flat tombstones of a now unused
Arab cemetery, while the camel-drivers were making
ready for our trial-trip. The litter itself was shaped
like the Noah's ark of our toy-shops, and painted
in the same brilliant colours of red and green. It
was hanging by poles and chains from the pack-
saddles of two camels, one in front, the other behind
it. The camels were now being elaborately adorned
with strings of shells and beads, with little tinkling
bells and long woollen tassels. We had another
engagement that morning, and would gladly have
dispensed with some of the finery, but such was the
fashion for camels when bearing a lady's litter, and
we had to wait patiently until the last shell was
adjusted to the owner's satisfaction. Unfortunately,
while so much attention was paid to the camels, the

litter itself had been forgotten. The steps were
missing, and when we had somehow been hoisted up
by the men, we found inside none of the carpets
and cushions that might have made it a comfortable
lounging place. We had to sit down flat on the
rough dusty boards, too low to look out, and yet
half choked by the sand that blew in from all sides
through the unshuttered and curtainless windows.
As, moreover, the uneven steps of the camels gave us
a presentiment of sea-sickness, we were glad to get
out again. Our morning's work, however, had not
been quite in vain ; we had given a welcome spectacle
to the idlers of the neighbourhood, who had collected
in considerable numbers, squatting with their pipes
on the sunny banks by the road-side, and watching
our proceedings with truly Oriental composure.

Meanwhile our dragoman had not only concluded
his treaties with sheikh and archbishop, but had also
engaged a cook and two other servants to minister
to our well-being in the desert. These important
additions to our party were introduced to us at
Aḥmed's own house, whither we drove one morning,
by special invitation, to make the acquaintance of his
wife. Though allowed by the Koran to have three
of them, he, like most respectable Egyptians of the
middle class, had contented himself with one; and
their union was a happy one (to judge from his
frequent allusions to his domestic affairs), though she
had borne him no children. He occupied a roomy
house on the outskirts of Cairo, with yards and stables

attached. The chief part of it seemed devoted to his trade as dragoman; the lower floors were full of tents and tent-furniture, saddles and saddle-bags, and he showed us with some pride the new blankets and table-cloths which he had bought expressly for our use. In one corner a narrow staircase led up to the women's apartment; it was well carpeted, and furnished with low cushioned couches along the walls, to which had been added a few chairs for the benefit of European visitors. Our gentlemen, of course, had to retire, before Aḥmed proceeded to show us his wife. She was indeed a beautiful thing to be shown: rather short and plump, but well shapen, with a clear complexion and liquid brown eyes, clad in a robe of ruby velvet, and half hidden in a transparent cloud of some soft, white, star-spangled material. Her gait was not graceful, probably encumbered by her draperies, and she made no attempt at conversation; but she was lovely to look at, as she sat on the divan by our side, smiling at her husband and well pleased with us, because we admired the many golden rings and bracelets with which she was adorned.

Coffee was brought before we took leave and went down again to inspect our servants. The cook, a fragile-looking old man, a Christian from the Lebanon, seemed hardly strong enough for such an undertaking, yet he bore the fatigue well, and proved a better cook than some of us had ever had in our English households. His two companions were stout and sturdy, one an Egyptian waiter from a hotel in Cairo, the

other a nigger boy from the Soudan. Aḥmed called
him his son, and somebody told us afterwards the
story of his adoption. Ahmed had travelled on the
Upper Nile, when his gun went off accidentally, and
grazed the head of a bystander. It was a narrow
escape, and Aḥmed, full of gratitude to Allah, prayed
for a special opportunity of pleasing Him in return
for His mercies lately vouchsafed to His servant. He
had hardly risen from his knees when he saw a little
slave ill-treated by his master. He bought the child,
declared it free, and brought it up as his own. We
often found this idea of doing God a service, of giving
Him a pleasure, connected with the simple faith of
otherwise untaught Muhammedans. A physician from
Manchester, an experienced oculist, and his wife, were
staying at the same hotel with us. They went about
among the poor people, and he cured or relieved
many cases of ophthalmia, without, of course, expect-
ing any return. The man who attended his donkey
on those occasions became warmly attached to him,
and expressed his admiration by saying to the
lady: 'Your husband, he very good man, he make
God very glad.' (I do not think any other praise
could have sounded sweeter in her ears.) We told
this simple story to several friends in Cambridge,
and Dr. Latham, of Trinity Hall, seeing its deeper
significance, has handed it down to posterity in
his beautiful and suggestive little book on the service
of angels.

At length the camels and the stores were ready;

they started on their march towards Suez, and we arranged to follow three days later by the railway that now connects Cairo with the canal.

This interval of comparative rest was most welcome to us. We returned calls, we made a few additions to our personal outfit, such as blue glasses, cork helmets and puggaries, to protect ourselves from sunstroke and ophthalmia ; we filled a large box with our purchases from the bazaars, with photographs and other little mementoes, and dispatched it to England ; and we wrote long letters to friends and relatives in different countries, for we did not expect to have any means of communication with the civilized world after entering the desert beyond the Red Sea.

On January 29 we left Cairo, and during the next hour we traversed the most fruitful part of Lower Egypt, where three successive harvests ripen from year to year. The fields were all green and golden with maize and lentils, with melons and cucumbers ; and the water-meadows full of kine, fat-fleshed and well-favoured. It is the Goshen of the Bible, and the names of the stations still reminded our philologians of places mentioned in Genesis and Exodus. Soon after we plunged into the desert, and we felt how hard it must have been for the Israelites to leave the fleshpots of Egypt. The sand was blown into ridges and hillocks not unlike the waves of the sea : only now and then, as we approached or crossed the Fresh Water Canal, did we see small patches of green. This

canal was in existence 2,000 years before Christ, and
it was retraced and restored not long ago, chiefly for
the benefit of the workers on the Suez Canal. The
stations now presented nothing but a few low huts—
but on one of the tall sign-posts we read in large
letters, Arabic and English, the name of Tel-el-Kebir.
It was strange to reflect on the cries of agony and
fury, on the slaughter and bloodshed that raged here
but a few years ago, now, when the moving sands of
the desert have effaced every trace of the struggle.
However, a handsome monument has been erected
at some distance from the station to mark the graves
of the British soldiers. At Ismailieh we touched the
Suez Canal; but a long line of telegraph poles above
the low buildings on the wharf was all we could see
from our windows.

We now turned sharp to the south, saw on our left
the shining waters of the Bitter Lake, and could trace
the canal itself by the clumps of trees on its banks
and by the tall masts and smoke-wreaths of passing
vessels. As soon as our train ran into the lively little
station at Suez, Aḥmed appeared at the carriage door
with his satellites; he took charge of our persons and
of our parcels, kept the baksheesh-crying crowd at
bay, and led us safely to the little inn (proudly styled
Hôtel de l'Orient), where lodging and dinner had been
prepared for us; and we gladly gave ourselves up to
his guidance with a comfortable feeling that, with so
competent a protector, we need take no further care
what we should eat, nor how we should proceed on

the morrow. The inn was kept by a polite little Greek ; its chief rooms opened into a kind of garden-square furnished with rough wooden tables and benches, and lit up at night by a few Chinese lanterns. Here we stayed that evening, busy in revising our saddle-bags and night-sacks. They were filled, for the greater part, with the necessary books—dictionaries, grammars, and Bibles in different languages, early fathers, catalogues of MSS., and other learned works. We restricted our wardrobe as much as possible, leaving every superfluous article in charge of the land-lord, who insisted on writing an elaborate receipt in modern Greek for everything entrusted to his care.

We bethought ourselves rather too late that it might be well to take some light literature, poetry or fiction, as a relief from harder studies in hot and weary hours. The Suez station has no bookstall, and the wisdom of the dragoman found its limit here ; but a native, loitering about the inn, caught some of our words ; he promised, with many sly winks and nods, to show us just what we wanted, and curiosity compelled us to go with him. In and out, through narrow lanes and tortuous passages, he led us into a dark inner room, and there, from under his mattress, from outer wrappings of blankets and camel-rugs, and from inner coverings of silver and tissue-paper, he produced a large folio Bible, with gaudy illustrations perhaps seventy or eighty years old. We could not make out where he got it from ; he could not read a word of it, but he admired the pictures. I need not say that we left him in undisturbed possession of his treasure, he was disappointed, poor man, but a little baksheesh makes up for many troubles.

Next morning we were astir betimes, going to see our caravan, which had arrived two days before us, and encamped at the foot of a sandy hill just outside

CAMEL-DRIVERS.

the town. Suez itself is not the busy and flourishing place we had imagined it to be from its position at the mouth of the great canal. It seems that the local magnates squabbled so much about the price of land and the fees for wharfage, that the company transferred office and landing-stage to Tufikieh, a village two miles to the south, and even there the traffic is considerably less since the canal was lighted by electricity, so that vessels can enter at all times without waiting for daylight outside. The importance of our camp, on the contrary, far exceeded our expectations. It was full of life, getting ready to move on. Over thirty camels being watered, saddled, or loaded, accompanied every process with the same snarling growl. The drivers, one to each camel, had been reinforced for the day by idlers from the town and by visitors from neighbouring tribes. Some had lit fires and were roasting coffee in shallow iron vessels, or baking flat unleavened cakes in the embers. Others, in excited groups, were fighting, with shrill voices and violent gestures, not for, but against the separate loads assigned to their camels. Each driver (in most cases also the owner) cried out that his beast was over-burdened, and swore, by Allah, that he would rather return to his tents than carry the allotted amount. We thought at first such a number of camels and men excessive for conveying seven travellers across the desert, but we altered our opinion on seeing the stores which we had to carry.

There were the water-casks, just filled with sweet water from the Ataka mountain, chained together (two and two) ready to be slung across the pack-saddles, curious erections not unlike the rough wooden frame-work of a high-pitched cottage-roof, but well adapted to the peculiar shape of the camel's back. There were flour-barrels, sacks of charcoal, and a portable cooking stove ; large crates full of live turkeys, chickens, and pigeons (over 200 of them), and special water-skins and bags of grain for their maintenance. One huge chest was filled with loaves hot from the baker's oven, another with the cook's stores of beans, lentils, and rice. Five tents with their long poles, folding bedsteads, boards and trestles for tables and chairs, and large rolls of mattresses and blankets, formed less weighty, but more unwieldy packages. Immense baskets with oranges, dates, and dried apricots were still coming in ; while large rope nets held no end of smaller boxes and hampers, and all the necessary utensils of a wandering household. To divide these miscellaneous goods into equal shares seemed a herculean labour; but Aḥmed and our old sheikh were up to the occasion, and by alternately coaxing, threatening, and bribing, they managed to satisfy the most jealous of drivers.

Meanwhile we were not allowed to be spectators only of this busy scene. Aḥmed wanted us to choose, each of us, our own camel, and the best-looking and lightest-stepping animals of the caravan were brought for our inspection. There is indeed a special breed of camels, trained for riding, that are used in the army and wherever speed is required, but as we had to keep with our tents we wanted no swifter steeds, and took to the common baggage camels and wooden saddles of the Bedouin. These saddles have two high pommels, one at the back, the other between the knees of the rider, who usually crosses his feet in front of it and rests them on the neck of the camel. But so broad is the back and so steady the gait of the animal that it is easy to turn from side to side without dismounting, and the tedium of a long journey is much relieved by a frequent change of position. Aḥmed had provided large saddle-cushions for us, securely fastened to the pommels, that made commodious seats, especially when complemented by our rugs and overcoats. We obediently tried two or three different camels and saddles, but, as we were quite ignorant of what constituted their good or bad points, we gladly assigned our right of selection to Aḥmed, who speedily found for each of us a camel, a saddle, and a man. We had to carry our own personal luggage, the driver's blanket or cloak, his leathern water-bottle and private store of bread and dates, besides a sack of beans for the camel, in case the scanty herbage of the desert should fail us. The men were bound to provide for themselves and their beasts; but Aḥmed knew how to keep them in good spirits by doles of tobacco and other timely additions to their comfort. The camels were to start at noon, going up two miles along the canal, to pass by the bridge there to the other side, whilst we sailed across the gulf, to rejoin them on the opposite shore.

One more walk through the picturesque little town, one more inquiry at the post-office, one more 'good-bye' wired to England, then we went down to the quay, where the sails were already set. A small crowd had assembled, idlers from three continents, in all kinds and stages of dress and of undress; and when they pushed us off from the blackened timbers of their little wharf, and exchanged guttural farewell greetings with our sailors, we felt as if they launched us from the shores of civilization into a fabulous sea.

ON THE ROAD TO MOUNT SINAI.

CHAPTER III

THE weather was beautiful beyond description, and the north wind drove our boat gently through the blue transparent waters. She was stoutly built, and would have won any race, if 'slow and steady' always fulfilled their ancient promise. Mount Ataka, near Suez, a well-known landmark far out at sea, stood forth boldly against the brilliant sky, and the chalk heights of the Tîh began to show above the low Asiatic shore. The entrance to the Suez Canal, marked by buoys on either side, is kept clear and deep by careful dredging ; otherwise this northern extremity of the Red Sea is very shallow, and when the tide is out only small boats can cross in safety. But we had wind and water in our favour, and sailed southward for several hours, thus shortening the ride to Ayin Musa (the Wells of Moses), where we had arranged to camp for the night. Our sailors reclined in a picturesque group near the stern, alternately lit up by flashes of sunshine, or thrown into shade by the flapping of the large brown sail ; while a red sash or bright yellow turban added beautiful bits of colour to

their swarthy faces and bronze-tinted limbs. Aḥmed
opened for the first time his tin box and large wicker-
covered flask, henceforth familiar features of our midday rest; he distributed cold chicken and hard-boiled
eggs, bread and cheese and oranges, and filled our tin
mugs with water and lemon-juice. We had been too
much absorbed by the novelty and strangeness of our
surroundings to think of eating and drinking; but he
knew what we wanted, and never was a meal more
enjoyed than this luncheon in the rough sailing-boat
on the Red Sea.

Towards three o'clock, or, as we had now to reckon
about the ninth hour, we landed at a little breakwater; the sailors laid our luggage down on the
beach and pushed off again, to reach Suez before
night. The breakwater was under repair, huge
timbers and heavy tools were lying about on the
sand, but the workmen had left for the day; the
camels were not in sight, and the dragoman went
in search of them. The soft splashing of the waves
on the lonely shore was the only sound we heard, as
we sat on our rugs and carpet-bags, and looked on the
desert in front of us. I do not know how long we
waited, but the sun neared the horizon; a cold wind
came in from the sea, and I confess that old stories of
hostile tribes and howling jackals began to arise in my
mind; at length Aḥmed returned, having met a messenger from the sheikh: the caravan had been delayed
at the bridge, and was still several miles behind us.
So we started on foot in the direction of the palm-

trees of Ayin Musa, whose tops we could discern in
the far distance, four or five miles inland.

This little oasis is the first resting-place of all caravans from Suez ; here the Israelites must have stopped
after their passage through the Red Sea ; and for the
next nine days we were to follow in their track.   For
the places where water can be found are few and far
between, and travelling here is only possible by taking

NEAR AYIN MUSA.

these same stations on the way : though the footsteps
of the camels are soon effaced by wind and sand,
they all take by instinct the straightest line from one
well to the other, and people meet face to face in
the pathless desert as if they were travelling on a

well-known road. The yellow sand under our feet
was pleasant to tread on, something like the gravel
on a garden-walk; the palms grew higher and higher
above the rosy horizon, and at dusk we reached the
fenced plantation of dates and bananas that still bears
the name of the great law-giver; the little hostelry
within consisted of low open sheds built round three
sides of a square; the middle part provided with
rough wooden benches for the reception of travellers;
the rest serving as warehouses or as a shelter for
animals. In times of unusual traffic belated guests
would naturally be relegated to these 'stables,' without any unkindness on the part of the host. We
found the place empty, but for an officious waiter,
who brought coffee and lit a large stable lantern that
swung from a hook in the ceiling. He was very
anxious the ladies should recline on his pillows, which
he heaped on the seats on one side of the shed. I am
afraid we seemed ungrateful, but we had good reasons
to prefer the bare boards at the further end. There
we huddled close together, and, instead of watching
eagerly for the first signs of the approaching caravan,
we forgot desert and oasis, and were overpowered by
sleep.

About an hour later we were roused by the wild
shouts of the Bedouin and the commanding tone of
Aḥmed's voice. Wide awake and leaning over the
fence at the end of the plantation, we seemed still to
be dreaming, so weird and fantastic was the scene we
had come out to witness. The full moon had risen,

and covered the desert with a silver sheen that con-
trasted strangely with the deep shade under the palm
trees and the lurid glare of the camp fires. The
camels, lying down between their burdens, seemed to
leave no room for the tents; the men, bewildered by
the lateness of the hour (they seldom travel after
sunset), and quite unused to the ways of civilized life,
stared in helpless wonder, or fell over each other in
their stretching of ropes and unrolling of carpets; the
tent-poles rose and fell like masts on a stormy sea,
the curtains flapped loose in the night air, and Aḥmed
threatened and thundered, trying in vain to keep each
man to his task : they would squat down in mute
contemplation, or rush wildly all together where only
one was wanted.

But while we still doubted whether food and rest
could ever be evolved from this chaos, one high pole
was firmly fixed, one white roof gleamed in the moon-
light, the sound of a gong called us to dinner, and the
waiter, with a stately bow, held the curtain aside, and
invited us to enter. The floor of the tent was covered
with matting, the table with a snow-white cloth, a large
bundle of flowers, bright candles, and vases of oranges
and pomegranates stood in the middle, together with
two clear glass flagons for the water, to convince us
of its purity. Though the plates and dishes were of
tin, they were neatly enamelled in white and pink,
and when excellent soup, meat, and pudding were
served in due succession, our rough cloaks and travelling caps seemed quite out of place at this well-

appointed table. Coffee was brought, the genuine coffee of Arabia, whose delicious aroma is elsewhere unknown; the beans themselves, freshly roasted and coarsely ground, fill about a third of the cup, but the clear liquid above is most refreshing and wholesome; it certainly never interfered with our sleep, though we took it every evening.

After dinner we read the history of the passage through the Red Sea from Exodus xiv; and then, though our watches only pointed to nine, we remembered that we were to continue our journey at sunrise next morning, and went out to look for our beds. All was now silent, the camels had been led aside to the fires, and were asleep, together with their drivers. Four smaller tents had been pitched for the night, and the place between them shone white and clear in the rays of the moon. My husband and I took formal possession of one of the tents; we found two camp bedsteads with a profusion of pillows and blankets, a board and trestles for a washstand, and a little carpet covering the remaining part of the sandy floor. Three large buttons and loops served as lock and key to secure the door of the tent, and soon we were warm asleep after this full day's excitement and fatigue. When we woke again, the dawn was stealing in overhead between the umbrella-shaped roof and the circular wall of our tent, and revealing the bright pattern on its curtains, quaint representations of palm branches and cherubim in red and yellow on a dark blue ground. A strange grumbling sound, like low thunder, reached us from afar; we knew it later on as the morning salute of our camels. Their peculiar hissing snarl, which seems at first to be the very essence of ill-temper and discontent, is much softened by distance; it is the only voice vouchsafed to these animals, and by no means always a sign of anger; they use it when meeting their friends, and when calling to their young.

Another sound, the clanging of the cook's soup ladle on a copper pan (last night's gong), roused us effectually from our meditations, and ere long we unbuttoned our curtains and looked on the glorious radiance of the opal sky, and on the boundless expanse of the desert. The sun was as yet below the horizon, and the sand had none of the dazzling glare that makes it later on trying to the eyes. The desert air in these early hours of the day has an indescribable charm, it exhilarates body and mind like new wine. However tired we might get in the noonday heat, or after a long evening's ride, every new morning brought us redoubled vigour and found us in jubilant spirits. A second application of the ladle told us breakfast was ready. It was well we had finished our toilet and restrapped our night-sack, for the Bedouin were already beginning to strike our tent. They worked with a will to-day; they had accepted once for all their appointed load, as they accept an irrevocable fate, and the business of packing went on in peace, with one single exception. Mr. Harris, who, as above mentioned, had joined us at Suez, brought from England an expensive photographic apparatus with all the latest improvements, packed in a separate box. Not wishing to carry this on his own came, he now ordered it to be sent on with the baggage ; but, though compared with water-casks and flour-barrels it looked no bigger than the proverbial fly on the camel's back, not one of the drivers would submit to the additional weight. We saw our personal property securely fastened to our saddles, Aḥmed helped us to mount, and himself led the way, leaving the sheikh to follow after striking the last of the tents. But still, as we left the camping ground, that unfortunate box was lying on the sand surrounded by six or seven black-bearded, rough-fisted men, and the disputes of the previous day seemed to be reviving. Somehow the difficulty was overcome, the box reached the next camp, and created no further disturbance ; but it is tragic to relate that this same camera, from a small flaw in its mechanism, proved utterly useless, while my own little Kodak, hanging lightly on my pommel, or on my shoulder, worked well, even in unskilful hands, and gave us many pleasant memorials of our expedition.

Having now fairly started on our ride across the desert, we had leisure to make the personal acquaintance of our camels and of their masters. My camel (Ahlan—that is 'Welcome,' by name) was the only white one in the caravan, rather old and heavy-limbed, but most sure-footed and steady. I got quite attached to it, and I fondly imagined that it returned my affection ; it certainly liked the bits of biscuit and sugar that I hid in my pocket surreptitiously after breakfast. The dragoman, while supplying our table most bountifully, was much averse to our giving away even a crust of bread to a beggar, or a bone to a stray dog ; I suppose he did not know the extent of our charity, and whether it might not involve him in serious difficulties, as he could not replenish his stores by the way. Our camels preferred walking in single file, never varying their long, measured stride, neither from fatigue, after three days' drought, nor from eagerness when water was near. They were guided by a rope tied loosely about their neck, and they obeyed their driver's voice in getting up and lying down ; but we ourselves, perched high on their backs, had no control over them, though we held the rope for hours together while the men fell behind to chat with their comrades. Now and then, when I found myself left in the rear, or wished to ride by the side of a companion, I managed to accelerate the pace for a moment by tapping my camel's neck with my boot as hard as I could ; but it soon relapsed into its own regular tempo of about three miles an hour. The only thing that ever disturbed its placidity, and made it swerve round with a violent jerk, was the sudden appearance of a round black shadow thrown by my sun-shade on the white sand just in front of us. Ibrahim, my man, seemed anxious to excuse his camel's naughtiness, and told me that it took the shadow for that of a panther, which animal some-

times lurks on the outskirts of an oasis, and has been
known once or twice in the memory of man to spring
on to the neck of a solitary camel. I did not know
enough Arabic to argue with him on the reasoning
powers of the animal's brain, but I was careful in
future, when opening my parasol, to avoid a similar
annoyance.

This Ibrahim, who, like the other drivers, made the
whole journey on foot, was a well-grown, stalwart
young fellow. I could not help admiring the beautiful
poise of his head, as he marched in front of me with
steps as firm and regular as those of the camel itself.
He was clad in a loose shirt and the usual inverted
sack of coarse indigo-blue canvas, probably woven
and dyed by the women of the tent, who had ornamented it in this case with a simple embroidery in
red wool along the seams. He had several coloured
handkerchiefs twisted round his head, and wore a long
sheathed knife in his belt, together with pipe and
tobacco-pouch. On the sands he walked barefoot,
but when we came to stony ground a pair of rough
wooden sandals was produced from one of the saddle-
bags ; in the same recess he kept several blankets or
wrappers, which he threw over his head and shoulders
one after the other as the day closed in, for warm as
the weather felt to our northern senses, it was the
winter season of the desert, and cold enough for the
natives.

Nearly the whole of our escort were armed with
long rusty guns, swords, daggers, or pistols, but their

weapons mostly reposed on the backs of the camels within reach of the riders. These Bedouin get part of their living by conducting travellers and merchandise across the desert between Suez and Petra; many of them also possess date-plantations in the oases or on the sea-board, and their camels and lean black goats provide them with milk and cheese, with fuel and clothing. My Ibrahim's home was in a moving camp not far from Ayin Musa, and he left us for two days to visit his family, entrusting the care of camel and rider to one of the camp-followers, who are never wanting on such an occasion. Most of the men were inveterate smokers, but they preferred to their time-honoured pipes the modern cigarettes of Cairo; and it was well for the general good-will of the company that we had brought a large boxful for their special benefit.

Our route lay to the south, crossing a wide headland that jutted for miles into the sea on our right. The sandy desert stretched all around without a sign of vegetation, except when we came to one of the shallow water-courses that carry from time to time the storm-water from the mountains down to the sea. They were quite dry now, and only marked by tufts of rough brown grass springing here and there from the barren soil, which our camels chewed with evident delight. It was difficult to believe that after the rare but furious rainfalls higher up, a stream rushes along here strong enough to overwhelm the camel and its rider; but caravans are warned against pitching their

E

tents in these hollows, as whole camps have been swept away by the sudden whirl of waters, that subsided again before the morning.

This being my first long ride, I found the constant swaying to and fro very trying, and I called several halts, to have my cushions moved, my straps tightened, or my stirrup adjusted; but these alterations caused a serious delay to the whole party. Aḥmed, in each case, had to be summoned from the front, and my camel took so much time, bending and unbending its long limbs, that I resolved to bear henceforth my discomfort in silence; however, I soon became used to this novel exercise. I learnt to dispose my rugs and pillows to the best advantage, and after a few days camel-riding seemed an easy and enjoyable pastime. But on this particular morning we were none of us sorry when we stopped for luncheon after a four hours' journey; the animals were left free to seek a mouthful of withered grass, the drivers crouched round a fire of camel-dung, and we arranged our saddles and coverlets as couches under the slope of a sand-ridge, sheltered our heads as best we might with our umbrellas, and dozed away the hottest hours of the day.

In the early part of the afternoon, with eyes only half open, we watched the long line of our baggage-train filing past; it had started several hours later, but was now going ahead to prepare a place for us in the wady (valley or watercourse) of Sadur. When Aḥmed called his party together to resume the ride, the shadows of the camels were beginning to lengthen, and the colours of earth and sky to soften and melt into a golden haze on the far-off horizon. There was no trace of life in the desert except here and there, half-buried in the sand, the snow-white skeleton of a camel that had fallen by the way. We plodded on patiently for ten miles more, until we saw our tents bathed in the last rays of the setting sun, with the dusky figures of the Arabs hovering in front, tightening the tent-pegs and levelling the sand. The cook met us with cups of fragrant coffee, and soon we were secluded within our curtains, removing dust and travel-stains, and 'dressing for dinner.' We knew that the water in our jugs must suffice for next morning's ablution, so we used it with care, and as the nights were cold at this time of the year, even in the desert, we put on our warmest cloaks and caps in preparation for the welcome sound of the gong.

The crowing of our cocks woke us very early next day, and we two were ready to start before the camels had been saddled. The balmy freshness of the morning sky, and the firm and even surface of the ground, tempted us to walk ahead by ourselves in the direction pointed out to us by one of the Bedouin, while Aḥmed was still engaged in the camp. The desert, as it stretches away into the distance, looks perfectly flat, and the hills on the farthest horizon stand out sharp and clear, appearing to English eyes much nearer than they are in reality. It seemed impossible that camels or men could escape

E 2

from sight in so open or level a plain, and we wandered leisurely along without dreaming of difficulty
or danger. But the occasional ridges and hillocks of
sand, shaped anew by every change of wind, and lost
to a general survey in their uniformity of whiteness
and glare, are yet high enough to hide man from man
within a hundred yards of each other.

We had not left the tents for more than ten minutes
when we turned to look for our companions ; we saw
nothing but sand. We called, and got no answer.
We would gladly have retraced our steps, but our feet
had left no marks on the gravelly soil, and we had not
experience enough to be guided by the sun. Turning
round and round, in the vain hope of discovering some
trace of camels or tents, we got quite bewildered as to
the direction in which we had come ; and we felt like
naughty children that have run away from their nurse
and do not know where to find her. We had not
gone far, and must be missed before long ; so there
was no serious cause for alarm, but we spent a disagreeable quarter of an hour, standing in the same
place, for fear of straying further away, and trying to
attract attention by waving our handkerchiefs and
shouting at intervals. The man who came in search
of us looked formidable enough with his long rusty
gun and glittering dagger, with his wild gesticulations
and unintelligible cries. To us he was as the angel
of Hagar.

We soon rejoined our caravan that had meanwhile
started from the camp in a different direction, listened

meekly to a lecture from the dragoman, and vowed
not to go out of his sight for the future. He spoke
to us in somewhat broken English, but he perfectly
understood all we said to him, and had moreover to
act as general interpreter, as our servants, the sheikh,
and the drivers spoke nothing but their native tongue,
in most cases a primitive unwritten dialect of Arabic,
peculiar to this part of the desert, of which our learned
gentlemen understood little more than their wives.
But being all eager to learn, we soon picked up the
most necessary words, and could ask for all we
wanted. However, Mrs. Burkitt, who had spent part
of her childhood in Beyrout, was the only one among
us who could really converse with the Bedouin ; she
got much amusing and interesting information from
them, and became a general favourite. They called
her ' Emira,' a princess. My husband, the oldest and
tallest of the party, was distinguished as ' Effendi,'
my lord. The rest of us passed simply as ladies
and merchants, ' Hawagy ' (the usual term for foreign
travellers in Egypt).

Our efforts at learning Arabic from the camel-men,
with all their amusing mistakes and misunderstand-
ings, proverbs, riddles, and songs, with now and then
a grave philological discussion, seemed to shorten the
long morning's ride that brought us to Amara (the
place of bitter waters, Exod. xv. 23) ; but as it had
not rained for many months the hollows were dry,
and the men clamoured to press on towards Ghurundel
(the ancient Elim), which they hoped to reach on the

morrow. So, as soon as the intense heat subsided a little, we mounted again, still riding southward, with distant glimpses of the dark blue sea, and even of the African mountains beyond. The shadows lengthened, the sun went down in a glory of purple and gold, and the moon rose above the white range of the Tih on our left, and still we went on. We had all dismounted, and enjoyed a walk in the delightful cool of the evening, but we did not know how far our vanguard might have pushed on in their desire for water, and it was weary work in the end to pass from one sand-hill to another, straining our eyes to discover the tents in the gloaming. Suddenly a bright star seemed to rise just in front of us, and a shout went up from our Arabs, ' The fire, the fire !' We were indeed close upon the camp, coffee was ready, and dinner in full preparation.

Our drinking water was not improved by three days' journey under a burning sun, and we were glad to-night to pass it through a filter and mix it with claret, of which we had fortunately brought a comfortable supply, on the advice of medical men. The water of the desert is neither palatable nor wholesome for people unaccustomed to the climate; the Bedouin, indeed, drink nothing else, though their imperfectly tanned water-skins give it at times a most unpleasant flavour. Muhammed forbade his followers all alcoholic liquors, and, as a rule, his precepts are kept to this day. There are, of course, exceptions, especially in Egypt, where the population is so largely mixed with foreign elements; but drunkenness, as a national vice, is unknown; and it was painful to hear a donkey-boy exclaim at a drunken soldier or sailor, ' He a Christian, he drink.' The missionaries do all they can to make their converts sober and temperate, in the highest sense of the words; but they regret sometimes that they cannot make total abstinence also a tenet of Christianity.

Hitherto we had met only a solitary Arab, whose camel carried charcoal from oasis to oasis; and a couple of half-naked children from a moving tent had scampered along with the camels, happy to get a few raisins or sweets for their trouble. But on approaching Ghurundel we espied a company of camels and men moving in our direction; they were yet a long way off when Mr. Burkitt, with sharp-sighted eyes, recognized the ruddy faces and trousered legs of European travellers. The English consul and the chaplain of Suez were returning from a holiday tour to Sinai, and soon we shook hands with them and exchanged eagerly our messages and news. Sitting down on the sand, we scribbled hasty lines to friends in Cairo and Cambridge, while they charged us with greetings to the monks of St. Catarina. We had a fortnight's political news to impart, while they gave us an account of their journey: they had found the top of the mountain covered with snow, and suffered so much from cold in their tents that they gladly accepted the rough hospitality of the convent walls; but as the weather had changed on the day when they left, we might hope for more favourable circumstances. Our fame had gone before us; the monks had not only heard of our intended visit, they also knew our successive camping grounds and the probable day of our arrival, and had even pointed out correctly to these travellers the very place where they would fall in with us. We only understood after several weeks at the convent the rapid and regular way in which the inmates receive all similar information. The incessant moving to and fro of families and tribes, their constant connexion with the convent, and the clear view obtained from the mountain-tops over the greater part of the peninsula, combined to make news travel fast in this country without roads, postmen, and telegraph wires.

With many good wishes on both sides we parted reluctantly from our countrymen, and soon came to look, in a wide basin between sandstone hills, for the twelve wells of water and the threescore and ten palm-trees of Elim. We lunched in the shade of a magnificent dom-palm, which, different from the date-palm with its long graceful leaves waving from the top of a slender stem, branches out from the roots and forms a compact mass of dark-green fan-shaped leaves, looking from afar like one of our large forest trees. The other palms, though their number exceeded that mentioned in Exodus, were mostly stunted, or still in their infancy, and many of the wells were dried up. We saw only one deep hole full of muddy water, not far from our palm-tree; it was

GROUP OF PALMS.

surrounded by a low wall and troughs of roughly hewn stone, and here the men were soon busy with ropes and pails drawing water for their camels. It was slow work, and no Rebecca came to assist them. The animals drank deliberately, two or three at a time, in long thirsty draughts, but apparently without hurry or greediness. There was enough for all, but the day was far spent when the caravan set off once more.

We followed about an hour later, and felt like coming home when, after a short and pleasant ride, we found in a sheltered hollow our tents pitched, our fires burning, and our table spread with all that hungry travellers could desire. The turkeys strutted about and the poultry crowed and cackled, glad to be released for awhile from their narrow cages ; I am afraid they had much to suffer during these first days of their journey, but as chicken, boiled, roasted, or made into soup, formed now the chief article of our diet, the survivors became day by day more comfortably housed.

Not having progressed far this day, we started all the earlier on the following morning. We had now crossed the open desert; we left the wilderness of the Tih to the east, and entered the sandstone region that forms a stepping-stone to the higher granite peaks of Horeb. The ridges of the previous day rose to overhanging cliffs; we rode, now through narrow defiles, now through open valleys in ever-varying scenery—steep hill-sides where the different strata

showed like bright-coloured ribbons, castle-shaped
rocks that seemed to bar our way, and distant
mountain-tops that beckoned us onward. A large
heap of loose stones right in the middle of our track
was greeted by the Arabs with loud execrations;
each man threw an additional stone on to the mound,
and wanted us to do the same. It is said to be the
grave of a beautiful horse spurred to death by its
master, Abu-Zennib: here it gave one last frantic
leap and fell down to die, many centuries ago; but
still passers-by remember the gallant steed and curse
its cruel rider. The broad valley, Shabêka, led us
once more towards the sea; we hoped to hold our
siesta lulled by the music of the waves, and to get
into the heart of the mountains before nightfall, but
we came to a premature stop. Mr. Harris, a good
pedestrian and an experienced traveller, was fond of
lingering behind or walking ahead by himself, keeping
out of sight longer than the dragoman liked. He
had been warned to be careful, and had hitherto
always rejoined us in good time without causing any
anxiety. But to-day he had left us soon after sunrise:
several hours had passed, the country became more
and more broken; we looked out for him from every
available vantage-ground, we shouted until we were
hoarse, but only the echo answered with mocking
distinctness. Ahmed, who had crossed the desert
many times, knew only too well its perils for the
solitary traveller: he was without water, no tribe
was likely to camp here for miles around, as an

exceptionally dry season had driven them all further to the south, and once off the chief track he would not meet any other traveller. At eleven o'clock a general halt was called. We sat down under a group of palms in a sheltered corner of the valley; Ahmed provided us with food and drink, then he and the drivers went off in different directions to make a regular search. I shall always remember as a nightmare those hours of waiting, and the dreadful pictures conjured up by our fears—a funeral in the desert, or a skeleton blanched by the tropical sun, like those of the poor camels we had seen the day before, and the agonizing letter to be written to his home. One man after the other returned without having found any trace of the missing traveller. A messenger was now dispatched to the sheikh, who was still some way in the rear, and all his men were ordered to scour the neighbouring hills. 'Find him we shall,' said Aḥmed; 'but shall we find him in time?' We were on the verge of despair when the last of our men came back with Mr. Harris by his side; he was not nearly so much exhausted as we had imagined, and did not seem to have wandered very far. We were all delighted to see him safe and sound, and by the afternoon we had all of us sufficiently recovered from anxiety and exertion to continue our journey.

From this valley of Shabêka two roads, or rather camel-tracks, branch off to meet again near the top of Mount Sinai: one turning to the left, or inland, reaches it from the north; the other, easier to ascend, and probably chosen by the children of Israel, leads first along the sea and then up on the western side of the mountain. The three days where we 'found no water' (Exod. xv. 22) were now lying behind us We had carried, besides our water-casks, a quantity of seltzer, but would hardly need this on the mountain, while we might find it useful when recrossing the plain; and as additional weight is always best avoided on a long journey, we made a hole in the sand near the junction of the valleys, at a prominent angle of the cliffs, under a certain juniper bush, and buried our bottles, in the hope of finding them again in the still thirstier weather of March. This done, we struck into the long Wady Tayyibeh (the Happy Valley) and made straight for the shore. The air quivered with heat, and the south wind felt like the breath of a furnace; but the sight of the dark blue sea, though yet miles ahead, seemed to cool the atmosphere around us.

We rode down along the slope of the Tayyibeh mountain, perforated by caves and sulphurous springs, and cleft into fantastical shapes. The waves wash its foot, but the tide was out, and we could pass between the rocks and the sea, while the camels, who prefer dry ground, found a path higher up on the face of the cliff. We cooled hands and faces in the transparent pools, fishing for strange shells and bits of white coral. The briny scent of the wet sands, and the spray of the breakers, were unspeakably refreshing after our hot ride. The African mountains showed

in graceful outlines on the opposite shore, undimmed
by a distance of over fifty miles, and a large steamer
from India left long silver furrows in the tranquil
sea. As we rounded the promontory, a wide plain
opened before our eyes, stretching far inland between
two ranges of sandstone hills; and beyond and above
we saw for the first time distinctly the goal of our
pilgrimage, the dark granite masses of the Sinaitic
group. The top of the holy mountain itself is not
often seen from afar, as it is surrounded by other
summits of similar size. But Mount Serbâl, its rival
in height and in holiness, lifts its proud serrated head
in majestic grandeur above its lower companions, and
formed henceforth a chief feature of our landscape.
We all regretted that the camels with the tents had
already gone up to camp in the valley, so that we
could not spend the night on the beach. The sea
never seemed more beautiful; no scientific reason
has ever been given why it here bears the surname
of ' Red,' but to-day, as its quiet mirror reflected the
splendour of the setting sun, it glowed indeed like
red wine, and gained a royal right to its title. Reluctantly we turned from the shore, and slowly ascending
rejoined our caravan.

We camped on open ground, still in the sight of
the sea, but when the next morning rose above Serbâl
we set our faces towards the sunny mountain-tops at
the head of the valley, and began in good earnest
our uphill work. The day became very hot, and it
was well that we carried water-flasks and lemon-

drops in our saddle-bags; the latter were an unknown luxury to the Arabs, and the smiles on their dark faces as they sucked those tiny sweets were pleasant to behold. The ground became rough and stony, but the camels never slackened their pace ; and when the shadow of a great rock in the wilderness invited us to our midday rest, we had left the hills far below us that stood last night about our tents. As we rode on after luncheon the valley narrowed into a mountain pass, leading now between high rocks, and now along the side of a cliff that descended unpleasantly steep on our left; the dragoman ordered every driver to keep close to his camel's head, and assured us that we were perfectly safe. Yet we did not feel comfortable on our high seats, jolted from side to side by the uneven steps of the animals when striding over a big boulder or turning a sharp corner of the cliff; we all desired to dismount, but it was not easy to find places wide and smooth enough for the camels to lie down, and it took some time before we were all securely deposited on our feet.

Half an hour's climb brought us to the top of the pass, and we looked back into the deep valley from which we had come, and far away over vast ranges of sandstone. Now and then they slope gently down in even layers, forming bands of exquisite colouring in different gradations of russet, slate-blue, and yellowish-brown along the steep banks of valley or ravine. In other places they have been broken through, and tossed about in gigantic disorder by the fiery action of volcanic masses that now rise high above them as dark cones of red or black granite. It was a grand sight, and taught us more of the Power that ' bringeth forth the mountains' than many printed pages of geology; but it lacked the winning beauty of our Alpine scenery; there was neither wood nor water, neither green pasture nor soft covering of snow; all was bare and dry. A few tufts of bedherân, a kind of fragrant heather, had sprung from the clefts of the rock during last year's rain; now they were brown and withered, yet they retained something of their pungent flavour; and even to this day, from between the leaves of my note-book, the little dry twigs greet me with the scent of the desert.

A slight descent on the other side brought us into the valley of Budhra, a mountain plain, strewn with huge boulders of granite, the relics of some ancient flood. A low rampart of light-coloured sandstone forms a kind of skirting to the darker heights on either side; it looks almost like the handiwork of giants, and on its stones, where they offer a flat surface easily accessible to passers-by, are found some of the so-called Sinaitic inscriptions. They were formerly believed, by certain scholars, to be relics of the ancient Israelites, and were expected to confirm, even to supplement, the history of their wanderings. They have now been proved to belong to a much later time. The learned Professor Euting of Strasburg, who studied here for several weeks, has tran-

F

scribed and translated most of them, showing them
to be of ante-Muhammedan, probably heathen, origin,
the work of traders who were in the habit of halting
here on their way from South Arabia. The inscriptions seem to date from the first six centuries of
our Christian era, and contain chiefly proper names
accompanied by short forms of blessings and the like.
They occur at longer or shorter intervals over a
distance of several miles, until the malleable sandstone recedes before the masterful granite. Low
cone-shaped hills separate Wady Budhra from Wady
Mokattab (the Written Valley), which is of similar
formation and interest.

Here we arranged to spend the following day,
Sunday, Feb. 5, a welcome rest for man and beast.
So our camp was pitched with more than ordinary
care : the five tents with their far-stretching ropes
formed a circle at the foot of a sheltering hill ; the
Union Jack was hoisted above the dining-tent, and
a strong pole in front of it bore a grand Chinese
lantern. The rest of the caravan retired to a respectful distance, where the voices of camels and men
would not disturb us, while yet the light of their
ever-burning fires cheered the darkness of the desert.
We had easily conformed to the dragoman's camp-
rules: we had risen every morning at half-past six,
breakfasted at seven, and lain down to sleep at noon ;
we had mounted and dismounted like good cavalry
soldiers at the first blast of the trumpet, and had
become fond of our camels and of our saddles. Yet

it was very sweet that Sunday morning to disregard the clanging of the saucepan, to turn in bed for another snooze, to dress leisurely without fear that an over-zealous Arab might suddenly begin to strike our tent, to be late for breakfast and still to sit down among the first. A flock of black goats came down from the neighbouring heights ; the herdsman had seen our caravan from afar, and was glad to exchange new milk for coffee and tobacco. With rugs and cushions we made comfortable seats outside the tents, shaded and fanned by the lazily flapping curtains. We had English prayers to read, Arabic prayers to learn, and prayers without any words to offer for our prosperous journey. Luncheon this day was a regular meal, daintily dished, and, as a pleasant surprise, Aḥmed summoned us to afternoon tea. This was not in the bond, but, knowing the weakness of English hearts, he had kindly substituted it for the cup of coffee which the law awarded us on travelling days when we reached the tents in the evening.

After tea we sauntered along the valley, and made afternoon calls by visiting our servants and our camel-drivers in their private domain. The cook, with great pride, led us to his kitchen, and exhibited his bright copper pans fitting into each other with movable handles, and his ingenious oven (of course of English manufacture), that turned out three meals a day for twelve hungry people, and yet could be telescoped and screwed into the smallest possible compass. We were more interested in his tiny charcoal pans sunk

F 2

in the sand, that kept a big kettle boiling for hours together, and in his delicate machinery for roasting, grinding, and boiling our beloved coffee, though we soon discovered that our Bedouin accomplished the same good result by feeding their fire with camel-dung, and by grinding their beans between two unhewn stones. Here we were by no means the only visitors.

We found that the news of our advent in Wady Mokattab had spread rapidly through this district of the Towara tribes : brothers and cousins of different degrees arrived to meet their relatives, whose blazing fires and full coffee-pots showed that the guests were not unexpected ; many of them had walked long distances, twenty or thirty miles, during the night. The friends saluted each other by laying hand in hand and temple to temple in a grave, affectionate manner : then followed the usual formulated questions as to each other's health and that of the family in the tent : the stranger sat himself down on a mat near the fire, and pipes, coffee, and story-telling went round as before his arrival. By far the oldest and most vener-able member of the whole company was our sheikh, though in his personal appearance perhaps the most neglected of all. He excelled in playing a kind of draughts, over which he seemed to spend the chief part of his time, beating all his less practised opponents. The squares were easily drawn on the sand, and the men consisted of white bits of quartz that abound in the desert, and of peculiar stones, black, hard, and

shiny—so we thought, but they were indeed little
pieces of dry camel-dung.

Our drivers varied very much in age, from grey-
bearded men down to mere striplings ; and one was
quite a child, only twelve years old, and not taller
than a well-grown English lad of ten. He was the
only son of a sheikh and, since his father's death,
nominal head of the family. He lived in the old
tent with his mother, but accompanied the men of
his tribe on their journeys, walking across the desert
at the rate of twenty miles a day. Mrs. Burkitt rode
on his camel; she understood his language, he could
talk to her of his mother and sister, and her kind
words soon gained the little fellow's heart. I have
seen him kiss her boot in dumb veneration ; it was
the only part of her dress he could reach with his lips
as she sat in the saddle. He was a brave, winsome
boy, still laughing and singing when others grew
languid and weary towards the end of the day.
I believe his whole wardrobe consisted of a longish
blouse or shirt that had once been white, and of
a little cotton skull-cap, but he marched proudly
along, and looked with the utmost disdain at some
little beggars that clamoured for baksheesh ; for was
not he the son of a sheikh and the possessor of a
camel ? The rough men were kind to him, let him
lie close to their fire at night, and covered him up
with their blankets. We were all inclined to pet him,
to let him ride on our camels, or to feed him with
dainties, but Ahmed warned us to be careful, lest we

should waken the envy and jealousy, 'the evil eye' of his companions.   Poor little Ayeed!

After exhibiting our scanty phrases of polite Arabic to the men we went on to the camels; their fore-legs had been chained together, that they should not disperse too far during this long day of freedom, and it was ludicrous to see the short, tripping steps of the usually so far-striding animals.   Slowly they approached from all sides of the valley, for it was supper time and their cloth was laid.   On separate pieces of sacking or canvas their rations of beans were measured out; each camel indeed knew its master's crib, or rather its master's discarded cloak; without sniffing or stooping they passed by many a tempting little heap, until in their own appointed place they folded their long legs for the night and began to munch with deliberate enjoyment.   We watched, each of us, our own camel, and would have liked to add a pail of water to its dry provender; but, though this was the third day since Ghurundel, we saw no sign of distress. Our own dinner was a sumptuous affair: excellent pea-soup (our cook was great in soups), roast turkey, and pigeon pie, with sundry sauces and compôtes, plum-pudding, tarts and jellies, and a profusion of fruit for dessert, very different from the orthodox cold-meat dinner of our Sundays at home ; but here with our troop of Muhammedan servants, we had no compunction on that point, and did full honour to the feast.   Before saying ' Good-night,' we read the seventeenth chapter of Exodus, in preparation for next

day's ride along Wady Feirân, which has been iden-
tified, with more certainty than almost any other
place in the peninsula, as the ancient Rephidim.

The wind changed during the night; it now blew
fresh from the north, and as we started while the
shadows of the hills were still lying across the plain,
we tightened our cloaks, and walked at a good pace
by the side of the camels, to keep ourselves warm;
but soon the sun proved conqueror, and the day
became quite hot enough for our comfort. This
valley of Feirân is over fourteen miles long, and
stretches, roughly speaking, from west to east, rising
slowly, but almost constantly, towards the centre
of the peninsula. Mount Serbâl, dark and majestic,
looks down upon it from the south, and endows the
lower part with its own character of barren solitude.
Its far-reaching outworks of steep rock, gigantic
boulder, and broken cliff make the approach to it
more difficult than the ascent; but this also must not
be attempted without the assistance of some neighbouring Bedouin. For though it stands only 8,000 feet
above the sea (much the same as Mount Sinai), its
granite walls and deep clefts are dangerous obstacles
for any one unacquainted with the locality.

Very different from this stony wilderness is the
large, fruitful oasis of Feirân, that occupies the upper
part of the valley. Here the mountain waters descend
as into a basin, fructify the soil, and then escape as
a sparkling rivulet that, a few miles lower down, is
lost again in the sand. The running water, the grace-

ful date-palms, flowering orchards, and fenced gardens were quite a novel sight after our seven days of desert life. Early Church history mentions bishops and even an archbishop of Feirân, and the crosses cut in the rocks above still mark the places where ancient hermits dwelt, while the ruins of chapels, towers, and fortifications on the surrounding heights show that the oasis was once the seat of a thriving population. At present the sparse inhabitants live in tents, in huts rudely built of unhewn stones, or between ruined walls thatched over with palm-branches. We saw great flights of pigeons, herds of sheep and goats, and droves of camels with their foals, beautiful little creatures with the mysterious charm that belongs to all things young, even when hump-backed. Children, half or entirely naked, ran in and out of the banana-groves, or peeped at us furtively from behind hedges of prickly pear, and a few men came to salute their cousins in our caravan. Otherwise the rich plantations seemed to be deserted by their owners.

Several tribes have their encampments here, but their nomadic instinct will not allow these people to settle quietly in any given place, however fertile and pleasant. The men prefer the freedom of the desert; they carry the products and simple manufactures of their oasis far away into Egypt and Palestine, and only return at stated seasons to gather in their crops or to rest a while from their travels. The celebrated dates of Feirân are here crushed and compounded to a firm dough, mixed with almonds and sewn tightly

up in pieces of skin in the shape of short thin
sausages. Thus prepared, they keep for years, are
most nutritious, and of excellent flavour. Cut into
slices they look like the well-known 'Cervelat-Wurst'
of Brunswick, and were easily mistaken for such by
friends who first saw them at our house in Cambridge.
Another product of Feirân is kamar-ed-deen (in
English, the moon of religion). This is a kind of
apricot marmalade, boiled a long time, then spread
and dried in thin layers on flat hot stones. It looks
and feels like coarse brown blotting-paper, and is of
all kinds of food the most portable. Like paper, it
can be folded up or torn into pieces and carried in
pocket or turban; but in the mouth it melts like
jelly, is meat and drink in one, and with its pleasant,
slightly acid taste, very refreshing in hot weather.
It is a great boon to the natives during the severe
fasts of Ramadan, being readily at hand whenever the
setting sun or the muezzin give the sign of reprieve.
Thence its otherwise incomprehensible name. Mats
and fans of palm-leaves are made here in great variety
and number, chiefly by the women and children; also
a special sort of saddle-bag, of rough camel-hair cloth
with bright embroideries in red and green wool, and
long tassels of the same material. Most of our camels
were furnished with these saddle-bags, and the tassels,
that almost touched the ground, made agreeable
handles for us when walking by the side, and helped
us to keep up with the long stride of the animals. This
is easy enough for a moderate walker, but if you once

allow yourself to fall behind, only for a minute, you cannot recover your place without a smart run, which is not convenient under an almost tropical sun.

Most travellers stop a few days in Feirân, to examine its ancient remains, and to make the ascent of Serbâl. But the nearer we got to Mount Sinai, the more intent we became on the work that awaited us there. We passed at dusk through the most interesting part of the valley, and encamped a little higher up, on a sandy flat. It seems natural that the Amalekites should have collected their forces in this neighbourhood, when bent on resisting the inroad of foreign tribes. Here they guarded the pass to the holy mountain, and here they held the water, whilst the host of Israel toiled up the long valley, murmuring against Moses. Our guides had pointed out to us, in the morning, the rock that Moses struck, and later on, that other rock, where Aaron and Hur upheld his hands: it was not surprising (to students of the Koran), but very pleasing, to see the veneration of these Arabs for Abraham and Moses, and for all the places connected with their history. Mount Sinai is sacred to them as to us, and the Christian monastery, in the shadow of that holiness, rests secure from any molestation.

Hitherto we had always pitched in the open desert, miles away from any human habitation. To-night we had neighbours, and they did not allow us to forget them. My pillow touched the outer curtain of the tent, and at midnight I was startled by the sharp cry

of a fowl close to my ear; it was repeated, feebler, in
the distance, and I concluded that a jackal was
making off with one of our hens, but a loud turmoil
arose of angry shouts and hurrying feet, of pistol-shots
and hoarse cries of 'Harami! harami!' i.e. robbers.
However, we had not much time to be alarmed;
Ahmed's reassuring voice called on us to keep quietly
in bed, and ere long everything was silent as before.
We had almost forgotten the disturbance of the
night, when at breakfast-time we found two young
ruffians tied to the lantern-post in front of the tents.
They were dressed, or rather draped, in the dirtiest
of blankets, and their scowling faces and long black
hair gave them a forbidding appearance; but, though
captured and kept for our inspection, they had not
been ill-treated; nay, even provided with hot coffee
and tobacco. These were only two out of a band of
five or six that had made a successful attack on our
poultry, on our loaves and oranges; but there was no
redress to be had, and by taking the law into our own
hands we should only make matters worse by bringing
on our defenceless heads the revengeful anger of
a whole tribe. Yet, to show these miscreants that
English travellers cannot be molested without some
inconvenience, Ahmed sent for their sheikh, an old
man with a most shrewd and wily expression on his
wrinkled countenance, and we were all drawn up as
in solemn conclave, looking as serious and wise as
possible, though at the time we understood little or
nothing of the proceedings.

Ahmed began by explaining to the sheikh that we were bound on a visit to his liege lord, the holy abbot of Sinai, who would look upon our affliction and replenish our wofully diminished stores, but would also warn all future travellers against employing the men or the camels of so treacherous a tribe. The sheikh then pleaded with many salaams that the culprits did not belong to his clan ; but, unfortunately for him, the prisoners had already claimed him as their uncle and protector. He next pleaded that nothing had been taken away, and that the whole affair was a vain alarm, caused by some boys who had lost their way among our tents. But as Ahmed stood firm and our solemn features did not relax, he came down, step by step, and ended by promising full restitution of our goods and dire punishment of the offenders, if only we would obtain for him a full pardon from the abbot. And so we parted, with many mutual compliments and vows of everlasting friendship, and went our ways, he arm-in-arm with his worthy nephews, rather proud of having attracted so much attention, and we poorer by a few loaves, but richer in memory by a most dramatic scene of life among the Bedouin.

As this sheikh felt himself answerable for the misdeeds of his people, so our sheikh had pledged his faith for the truth and honesty of his followers, and we had learned by this time that we could trust them implicitly. We had no doors to lock, no boxes to shut ; we slept soundly all night, our saddle-bags

were often left outside the tents, and all stores were
at the mercy of the drivers, yet not the smallest thing
did we lose during two months of this out-of-door
life. I broke my comb, and, possessing a dupli-
cate, threw away the pieces before leaving the camp;
they were brought back to me at night by one of
the attendants! Yet, with all this loyalty towards
us, whom they had taken under their special protection and guardianship, I have no doubt that the same
men, under different circumstances, might become
dangerous enemies to unwary travellers. Poor
Professor Palmer, one of my husband's predecessors
at Cambridge, was treacherously murdered in the
Peninsula, in 1882, probably by men of the Towara
tribe. But he was travelling in the interests of the
British Government, on a political mission, and was
known to carry a large sum of money on his person.

Between two prominent cliffs, as by a wide gate,
we left the beautiful valley of Feirân and came to
an open hill-side with tufts of bedherân and of a low,
leafless shrub with white thorns, three or four inches
in length. We had left Serbâl a good way behind us,
yet its proud, well-known head kept full in view, while
the much nearer summit of Sinai was still hidden from
our eyes by the rising ground in front. We were now
4,000 feet above the sea, and a keen mountain-breeze
tempered the heat; we hardly felt the fatigue of this
long day's ride, which brought us to the foot of
a steep pass, called 'The Pass of the Winds.' Here
we camped for the last time in company with our

camels. As a farewell present for their drivers, Aḥmed had bought a sheep at Feirân, and had carried it so far on his camel. It was now handed to the men, and they at once proceeded, in childish glee, to prepare it for their supper. They seldom taste meat, but live chiefly on bread and dates, and on the milk and cheese from their flocks. The 'kid from the goats' and 'the fatted calf' are regarded as luxuries now, as in the times of Abraham and of the prodigal son, and are only killed for honoured guests or on festal occasions. We heard their shouts and their laughter far into the night, and they let nothing of it remain until the morning, save the black fleece, which was to make a new cloak for their sheikh, without any help from the tailor's art. Several of the men possessed already such garments, and the fore-feet, with the hoofs left on, made convenient strings for fastening it around the neck. Soon after breakfast we began to ascend on foot the last granite ridge that separated us from the holy mountain. The pass was not nearly so difficult as it had looked from below ; it seemed to be quite a frequented road for this part of the world, and the camels followed us with ease.

We sat resting some time on a block of ancient lava, looking down on a little oasis far, far down below us, like a bright green gem in the roughest of settings. About ten o'clock we emerged on a wide, oblong plain, three or four miles in extent, between volcanic hills ; it was a barren desert without shade or vegetation, but at its further end, right opposite to where we stood, rose a cone-shaped mass of dark-red granite, 3,000 feet above the plain, so abruptly that the warning, 'not to touch the mountain,' seemed easy to understand ; deep rocky valleys on either side separated it from other summits of inferior height, and there, some way up in the valley on the left, we could just discern the dark walls of the monastery, built like an eagle's nest on a narrow ledge of the holy mountain.

CHAPTER IV

THE early history of the monastery of St. Catarina is difficult to trace. According to old legends and inscriptions the Emperor Justinian, about 530, built the outer walls—strong walls of granite, 20–30 feet high, and forming an irregular square some 200 feet in extent. There are but a few narrow windows or loopholes; sixty years ago there was not even a door, but visitors and monks alike were hoisted in large baskets to an opening in the upper part of the wall. The place was evidently built as a stronghold to defend the pass, leading from the plain of Er-Rakkeh in the north (where the children of Israel are said to have encamped) across a shoulder of the mountains into the Wady Tarfa, that slopes gently down to the south. It was first occupied by a garrison of Roman soldiers, sent to protect from savage Saracen tribes the inmates of an earlier monastery, dedicated to the Virgin Mary, higher up in the mountain, and the pilgrims and anchorites that flocked hither from Egypt and Syria during the early centuries of the Christian era; though, strangely enough, in the whole course of the Old Testament the prophet Elijah alone is mentioned as having visited this scene of the earlier dispensation. A grotesque old picture in the archbishop's room represents Mount Sinai as covered by monastic buildings in the shape of mediaeval castles half as high as the mountain itself.

Certain it is that the very inhospitality of these sacred rocks proved attractive to the religious mind. Hundreds of hermits lived and died here, dwelling alone in solitary caves, or gathering in groups at the feet of favourite preachers, in sheltered hollows, where the waters are held as in natural cisterns and reservoirs after the heavy rainfalls or snowstorms that occur here, at the best, two or three times a year, and where the traces of human habitation still survive in rude stepping-stones or in a few straggling fruit-trees of foreign importation. When the flourishing Christian community in Feirân declined, through heresies within and persecutions without, many of its members retired to the secluded wilderness of Sinai; and this became, before the time of Muhammed, the chief seat of Christianity in the peninsula. Yet it was not exempt from persecution. Many were the martyrs under Diocletian and Maximinus; later on the untutored Saracens carried on the work of murder and rapine, and the substantial walls of Justinian became a welcome city of refuge. Even the monks of the Virgin descended from their eyrie and, probably at this time, transferred to safer precincts their site of the burning bush. It is cherished to this day under

G

the roof of the church, but in closer proximity to the well of Jethro than is quite consistent with the biblical narrative.

And here the monastery grew and flourished. It counted from 300 to 400 inmates, who, with infinite patience in planting and irrigating, transformed the stony slope of the mountain into terraced gardens and orchards; it was visited by princes and emperors, and endowed with lands and dependents; it had colonies of its own order in Egypt and Russia and in the islands of Greece; its richly decorated church, though hardly founded by Justinian himself, as some chroniclers assert, was built not many years later, and its abbot received the dignity of archbishop, though nominally subject to the Metropolitan of Jerusalem. A new odour of sanctity arose in the ninth century with the legend that the body of St. Catarina, said to have died on the wheel (in 312), had been carried by angels to this Mountain of Sinai. It is difficult to connect the virgin-martyr of Alexandria with the bones which the monks disinterred here so many hundred years later; yet there is the fact that she became the favourite saint of the Eastern Church, and that her supposed remains lie in a beautiful marble sarcophagus in the church of the monastery on Mount Sinai, which has now for more than a thousand years borne the name of St. Catarina, though the original foundation was dedicated to the Virgin Mary, and the church itself built in memory of the Transfiguration.

The great wave of Muhammedan conquest that swept the adjacent lands, and made all their inhabitants submit to the sword or the Koran, did not interfere with the monks on Sinai. Rendered cautious by the history of former persecutions, they had become wise in their generation, and managed somehow to conciliate the powerful Prophet and to keep on friendly terms with his successors. Tradition tells us that Muhammed in early years, when on a pilgrimage to the Mountain of Moses, was kindly entertained by the monks, who later on, in memory of such hospitality, obtained from him a formal letter of protection, signed by his own hand with a broad black mark (for Muhammed, in all his wisdom, could neither read nor write). This letter acted as a talisman in keeping off invasion and pillage. Sultan Selim, it is said, carried off this precious document to keep as a curiosity with other ancient relics, but left an authenticated copy with the monks. This also has disappeared, but a second later copy is still shown at the Greek monastery in Cairo. In modern times the safety of the monks is guaranteed by a special charter signed anew by every Sultan of Constantinople. Baldwin, the short-lived King of Jerusalem, intended to visit the shrine of the burning bush, but was dissuaded by its clever custodians, who feared to provoke the fanaticism of the surrounding Saracen tribes. Such careful policy accounts also for the strange presence of a mosque within the convent walls. Some say that its erection was due

to the consideration of the monks for their Muhammedan servants, or to their preparations for a visit
from Saladin. But as we find it mentioned already
in 812, it was more likely the outcome of some early
compromise with the advancing forces of Islam.

However that may have been, the monks of
St. Catarina remained undisturbed in their mountain
fastness. Their numbers have gone down to forty or
fifty, many of their lands have been alienated, but
otherwise the inner constitution and the outward
appearance of the monastery are not much different
now from what they were 1,000 years ago. The
same rites have been performed and the same prayers
recited, day by day and night by night; still the
church and the mosque stand peacefully side by side,
and only their perforated tower and snow-white dome
are seen above the high outer walls as we ride slowly
across the plain of Er-Rakkeh. The holy mountain,
a plain, bare cone, as it first came into view, began
soon to show its deep vertical clefts and towering
rocks, until it looked, as we drew nearer, like several
peaks welded and hammered into one, while now
and then a gnarled olive-tree or a dark cypress told
of hidden springs trickling from the riven granite.

Wady-ed-Deir (the Valley of the Convent), towards
which we now wended our way, is a narrow gorge,
whose sides appear to have been torn asunder by
an earthquake. Large masses of rock have fallen
down, almost blocking the pass, and balanced one
upon the other as if ready to crush the intruding

traveller. On our left we looked down a wide valley (Wady-es-Sheikh), part of the second caravan route from Ghurundel. Compared with the wild scenery in front of us this seemed quite a hospitable region, the sides less steep, and the flat sandy bottom relieved by scattered tufts of herbage and by a browsing flock of lean black goats. Like a sentry-box at the entrance of the valley stood a solitary hut on a rocky, circular mound : four rough stone walls, with shutterless openings for window and door. It was erected as a shelter for Captain Palmer during his survey of Sinai, and long after the storms have swept it away, the name of ' Palmer's hill,' which the natives have given to the mound, will perpetuate his memory in the desert. Not far from it is a Bedouin burial-place, unspeakably dreary and sad : a low wall of loose stones, pretending to keep out the jackals ; a few flat, irregular tombstones, without any attempt at ornamentation or inscription ; and, as the only sign of loving thought for the dead, a few dry sticks, once palm-branches, planted at the head of a little grave in the remotest corner [1]. Another similar wall, but higher and stronger, surrounds about half an acre of ground just at the

---

[1] There are other old burial-places in the Peninsula, built of hewn stone and shaped like beehives. Travellers say they are called *Nawâmîs*, which means ' gnats,' and an absurd story is said to be current among the Bedouin to the effect that the children of Israel built them as a shelter against a plague of gnats. But our men assured us that these stone beehives are still in some cases used as tombs. I am certain that the word is not *Nawâmîs* (gnats), but *Nawâwîs* (shrines), plural of *nâ'ûs*, an Arabic word derived from the Greek *ναός*, and actually used of the Parsee ' Towers of Silence.'—F. C. B.

foot of Wady-ed-Deir, a resting-place for caravans that have not, like ourselves, obtained permission to camp within the grounds of the convent. The path up the valley, well trodden by camels and men, resembled, now a gravel walk, now a rocky stairway or a deep sandy track; only once, for about fifty yards, it widened into a well-paved road, probably the remains of a never-finished avenue, planned in remote ages in expectation of some distinguished pilgrim to Sinai.

At length our ten days' journey across the desert was accomplished. We had made the last stage of it on foot, and as the valley got a little broader we came up unto a kind of natural platform, just opposite to the walls of the monastery. They looked nearly as old and forbidding as the mighty mountain itself that towered beyond in almost perpendicular cliffs; but at their feet the wilderness blossomed indeed as a rose—almond-trees in fullest flower, olives with their tender bluish foliage, and cypresses in darkest green, clothed the orchards in a wealth and variety of colour that hardly needed the sombre background of granite to make a perfect picture for the painter's eye. 'All the trees of the world grow in the convent-garden'; thus little Ayeed had told us in childish admiration. Certainly all the beauty that trees can give to a barren land were present in this place.

Our dragoman was at once admitted by a heavy wooden gate into some outer court; he went to present our credentials to the porter and the steward,

while we sat on the rocks outside, waiting, full of awe
and curiosity. Between us and the ancient walls was
first a rough road, and then a large covered well or
cistern ; its low stone roof sloped to the ground, and
a dark flight of stairs went down as into a vault.
Here several men were busy fetching water or per-
forming their ablutions, apparently quite unconcerned
about the arrival of strangers. But a group of scantily
clothed children watched our every movement with
beautiful wondering eyes, not, I am afraid, without
a view to future baksheesh. When Aḥmed returned,
he was accompanied by a monk, who beckoned us to
enter. The court was occupied by different sheds or
outbuildings. On the right some stone steps descended into the gardens, while on the left a low
evidently modern gateway led into the convent itself.
Here we were welcomed by the steward, a handsome,
intelligent man, in a few words of fluent French,
intimating that the abbot (or, more correctly, the
locum tenens of the abbot-archbishop, who resides
for the greater part of the year in Cairo) was ready
to receive us. We had to stoop in the dark, narrow
passage through the massive wall, that brought us
into one of the inner courts. The ground here was
very uneven, for we stood on the slope of the mountain, and rock-hewn steps, worn by the feet of many
centuries, led up and down wherever we turned.

The buildings themselves, erected in different ages
and for different purposes, are most irregular : strong
vaulted rooms built against the outer wall, rough

wooden galleries, little upper chambers high on the roof, hidden oratories, and a splendid church. But of all this we saw little during that first visit. Our minds were occupied, oppressed, by the traditions of the place. We stood on sacred ground, in one of the oldest strongholds of our faith; the man we were going to meet was a link of the chain, a member of the long line of hermits, preachers, and martyrs, of scribes, abbots and bishops, who have handed down to our days the light of Christianity in the desert; and he was in his own person the highest dignitary of the Holy Catholic Church in this wide Muhammedan district. Had the rules of the convent required it, we would willingly have knelt on his threshold or kissed the hem of his garment ; but our pious exaltation was doomed to some disappointment. A stout, red-faced monk, in the plain black garb of the Greek priesthood (rather greasy in this case), rushed forth with loud shouts of merriment, and fell on the neck of Mrs. Lewis, with whom he had made friends during the previous winter. He patted her affectionately, he felt her garments, he made her sit by his side with his arm round her shoulders. A lively conversation then followed in modern Greek, of which we understood nothing, but frequent bursts of laughter showed it to be of a very pleasant nature. The room was comfortably furnished, though, of course, without glass to the windows, and several young monks watched this unecclesiastical mode of reception with unmoved faces. We tried to do the same. His excessive friendliness augured well for his readiness in producing his literary treasures. The good old man had to be propitiated, yet we did not relish the thought that we might have to submit, in our turn, to similar familiarities. However, we were dismissed with a gracious shake of the hand, after partaking of some delicious quince-jam, that was served in a beautiful glass bowl, with a silver spoon for each guest.

We now retired to the gardens, or rather to a long narrow field planted with olives, that had been set apart for our use. It was separated by walled embankments from other terraces and plantations, and at its lower end stood the mortuary chapel of the monks, a plain whitewashed building with a little belfry on the top. Where the trees grew highest, on the side next the convent, was a well of crystal-clear water, surrounded by the usual low wall and drinking-troughs for the cattle ; above it, four stone piers with solid arches of masonry formed a kind of primitive temple, and here we rested during the heat of the day. In the afternoon the abbot (*hegoumenos*) invited us to a second interview, in order to show us the books. So, at the eighth hour (2 p.m.) we went, as before, to his private room. We had waited there some time, when we heard hasty steps, a fall, a cry, and the poor man came in with bleeding face and dishevelled hair. He had slipped on the stairs, and struck his temple against a sharp corner. But, though much shaken, he would not hear of dismissing us, but led, with grotesquely bandaged head, the way to his library. It contained, on orderly shelves, from 800 to 900 mostly printed books—Bibles, homilies, and prayer-books in Arabic, Greek, and Latin, works on history and biography, and a few volumes of travels. Perhaps the most important book in the room was a facsimile copy of the great Codex Sinaiticus, presented by Professor Tischendorf in place of the original MS., which he discovered here in some forgotten corner (in 1844). He carried it away with him as a loan, and persuaded the monks later on to give it as a precious offering to the head of their Church, the emperor at St. Petersburg, where it is now carefully preserved, ranking with the Codex Vaticanus as one of the earliest documents of Christianity. But neither Tischendorf's codex nor any of the other MSS. transcribed or collected here by the learned monks of bygone centuries were ever kept in this so-called library. At the time of our visit they were huddled together in large chests in a dark, musty closet, off the archbishop's room, a large, lofty apartment, used as the metropolitan's judgement-hall during his annual visits to Sinai, and that sanctuary was not to be opened before the following day.

When we returned to the garden the sun had disappeared behind the mountain, though it was still some hours before sunset ; the baggage-train had not arrived ; a chilly wind crept up the valley, and our corner near the well had become cold and comfortless. We sat close together, trying in vain to keep warm, and our spirits sank very low—by a natural reaction after the excitement of the morning. Ahmed tried story-telling, we even began a round game, but nothing availed until the growling of our camels in the yard above suddenly revived us. The men had been well schooled during the march. There were none of the wild scenes like those at Ayin-Musa,

THE CONVENT, FROM THE GARDEN.

each man knew which bale to undo and which rope to fasten ; and in a time that seemed incredibly short, even to our weary limbs and impatient stomachs, the tents were pitched and the coffee-cups filled. The cook was not long over his preparations for dinner, and the reading of Exodus xix made a fitting conclusion to this memorable day.

Next morning the poor old abbot was not well enough to receive us, and we went instead to take leave of our Bedouin and our camels. They had camped by the well outside, and were now returning to their tents and their pastures. They readily agreed to come again in a month from this time to carry us back to Suez; yet, as we watched them going down the narrow valley, one by one, the ships of the desert that had brought us to this rocky island, we felt, for the moment, like stranded sailors without the means of getting home again. Except during stated hours of divine service, the convent gate was open from morning till night, and we found our way under dark archways, on different levels, from one narrow court into the other. The old well, with its heavy stone roof and large windlass, is pointed out as the place where Moses helped the daughters of Jethro to water their flocks. There are little beds of herbs in sunny corners, and the bare stems of two or three cypresses have grown to an immense height, in order to lift their green heads beyond three-storied buildings and overhanging galleries into the free mountain air.

When one of the black-robed monks met us, he bowed his head and passed quietly by with a murmured blessing. But as we descended the wide steps that lead from a higher court towards the beautifully carved portal of the church, a verger or sacristan signed to us to enter, and presently we were joined by Nicodemus, the steward, with whom

we could freely converse in French, and who made
a capital guide. The church is an early Christian
basilica, and a good example of Byzantine architec-
ture. The outside is plain and insignificant, hardly
distinguishable from the other buildings that hem
it in or lean against it. But the interior, richly
decorated and in excellent preservation, is in strange
contrast with the nakedness of the land, and with
the mouldering cells and primitive habits of the
monks. Massive pillars of granite with foliated
capitals divide the nave from the low aisles, which are,
each of them, lighted by five long, narrow windows,
and contain several oratories and chapels dedicated to
different saints. Between the columns are old wooden
stalls, on the left a kind of pulpit, and on the right
the bishop's throne. The carving is somewhat heavy
and clumsy, yet not without interest. One of the
panels represents a model of the convent, held up
by Moses and St. Catarina; others commemorate
ancient bishops and benefactors. The raised platform of the choir comes out some way beyond the
wooden screen with its gigantic crucifix, and the altar
stands in front of the screen, as it were in the shadow
of the cross. The pavement of red and black marble
is modern throughout, but from the ceiling hang
a hundred antique lamps, of silver or beaten brass,
all different in size and shape; some are ornamented with ostrich eggs, others with silver doves,
joining their wings in a circle and carrying the lights
on their heads. Though the church, according to

Eastern custom, is overladen with painting and gild-
ing (even the granite columns are painted green), with
pictures and hangings and tapestries, yet the effect
of the whole is more solemn than gaudy. The upper
part of the apse or choir is filled with beautiful
mosaics of the seventh or eighth century, equal to
those in the churches of Italy. The chief space is
given to the scene of the Transfiguration, while Moses
before the burning bush, and Elijah, the prophet
of Horeb, occupy other prominent places; and
St. Catarina, martyred on the wheel, carried by the
angels or crowned by the Virgin, occurs again and
again in woodwork, painting and embroidery. Her
marble sarcophagus stands in the midst of the choir;
a smaller one, entirely of silver, was presented by
the Empress Catarina the Great, and there are many
other precious offerings in honour of the saint. Four
regular services are daily held in the nave (two of
them during the night), besides other rites performed
before particular shrines.

Of these, by far the most holy, the great sanctuary
in fact of the church on Mount Sinai, is the chapel
of the burning bush, at the back of the apse. Going
down a few steps, we came first into a little lobby,
provided with a comfortable armchair and footstool.
Here we sat down, one after the other, to take off
our shoes; then Nicodemus unlocked the door and
allowed us to enter. The room is about ten feet
square, the floor covered with a thick carpet, the
walls with old porcelain tiles of a soft blue tint, and

the panels of the door with mosaics in ivory and gold. In the outer wall, high up, is a square window with dim panes of glass, and beneath it a little altar (rather an open shrine). Three silver lamps, always burning, hang inside, and a plate of solid silver is let into the floor below, to mark the site of the burning bush. The cross on the altar, of exquisite workmanship, is a gift from the Emperor of Russia. Nicodemus took it down, and even gave it into our hands, that we might examine the delicate details : the artistic figures in the small enamelled medallions, and the jewelled initials of St. Catarina that are skilfully interwoven with the arabesque tracery. Perhaps in our eyes the impressive beauty of the chapel was a little marred by the grotesque old pictures, chiefly of apostles and martyrs, that abound on the walls ; but the monks admire it all the more for these pious additions, many of which are, moreover, long-cherished presents from illustrious pilgrims. Not only this particular place, but everything else in the church is kept with the greatest care, and the good fathers do not allow rust and moth to corrupt their treasures.

It is different with the mosque that stands close by ; though substantially built, it looks unused and neglected. The Bedouin that pass with their camels, though allowed to enter, prefer to say their prayers outside, and the flat roof of the well by the roadside seems to be a favourite place, where they spread their little mats and perform their devotions after washing in the water below.

At last, on the afternoon of Feb. 9, the abbot met us in the archbishop's room, and the palimpsest was brought out from its secret hiding-place. The photographs, taken by Mrs. Lewis, were excellent indeed of their kind. The book was much larger in size, and the underwriting, from its yellowish tinge, more easily distinguished from the clear, black characters of the later work; but the Gospels looked very faint and forlorn; their washed-out remains were partly, often entirely, covered by the female martyrology, written ruthlessly across them by the vigorous hand of some devout and, no doubt, well-meaning scribe; and it seemed at first sight as if little more could be recovered from the original than from those photographs. Yet the almost complete edition of *The Four Gospels in Syriac transcribed from the Sinaitic Palimpsest*, published by the Cambridge University Press in 1894, has since shown to the world how many difficulties can be overcome by true scholarship, self-devotion, and unremitting labour.

The archbishop's room not being always accessible, the precious volume was at once transferred—in the custody of a monk—to an upper chamber, opening from the wooden gallery at the top of the building; and the narrow window not admitting sufficient light, a rickety table was pushed out on to the gallery itself; and here my husband sat down, the first to attempt the deciphering of this almost illegible MS. A strong wind was blowing, flustering the leaves and chilling the reader, but he worked quietly on until the monk on duty told us that it was 'eleven' (5 p.m. according to *our* chronology), 'and therefore time to shut the convent gate for the night.' By the kind interference of Mrs. Lewis, whose every request the abbot seemed ready to grant, the book was henceforth entrusted entirely to the care of our party. It was taken down to the gardens and kept in the tents, and the work was considerably lightened by thus putting the time and place of it at the command of the transcribers.

H

CHAPTER V

OUR LIFE IN THE GARDEN

THE treasure for whose sake we had come so far was now in our midst, and it naturally became the pivot on which our daily life revolved. The perfect light of that cloudless sky was essential to the work; in the misty atmosphere of England it would have been impossible, and the very best artificial light (we had only two candlesticks between us) would not have sufficed. Professor Bensly, Mr. Burkitt, and Mr. Harris divided their nine or ten hours of daylight into three regular watches, and the work of recovering the obliterated text went on without intermission. Quite early in the morning one of our washstands was raised to the dignity of writing-desk, it was put in the garden to catch the first rays of the sun, and the book was taken out of the silken cover in which we enveloped it every night. Mostly my husband undertook the first watch, wrapped in his great-coat, with comforter and woollen gloves, for the nights were still frosty in February. A kind of hallowed circle was kept around that little table all day, where no interruption was allowed to intrude, though loving hands

were ever ready to sharpen the pencil or re-fill the
inkstand, to hold down the leaves when the wind was
high, or reach Bibles and dictionaries that found no
room on the narrow board. Our servants soon felt
the importance of the task: early coffee and extra
meals were willingly prepared for the faithful work-

TRANSCRIBING THE PALIMPSEST IN THE GARDEN.

man who had to forgo the family breakfast or
luncheon. The monks, when they passed through
our grounds to their lower plantations and gardens,
looked wonderingly at these wizards from the North,
who paid so much attention to the yellow parchments
which their owners could neither read nor appreciate.

Now and then one of them stood with bated breath behind the chair and watched the pen of the ready writer ; but neither servant nor monk dared speak to the student on duty, any more than on shipboard to the man at the wheel. Meanwhile the dragoman, the cook, and the waiters had settled comfortably in the corner near the well ; they had worked hard for us during the journey, hardest after reaching the tents in the evening, when they too were tired by riding all day. But here Aḥmed increased his staff by an elderly Arab who acted as kitchen-maid, and by an impish little boy who was supposed to look after the poultry, and they all enjoyed many hours of ideal Oriental repose by sitting cross-legged on their mats and smoking their pipes in the sunshine. Our turkeys and chickens also led a pleasurable life in the orchard, where abundance of last year's olives was to be found by scraping in the dry and sunny soil. They fattened visibly, and there was no lack of new-laid eggs for the breakfast-table. Our tents, no longer struck every morning, assumed more civilized manners : they stood facing each other, with an open space in the midst that was levelled and swept with scrupulous care by the black son of Aḥmed ; our clothes and books, instead of being crammed into saddle-bags and strewn about the floor, were neatly arranged on hooks around the tent, or piled on rush-bottomed chairs, which the monks had kindly added to our scant stock of furniture. The large bread-chest, with a red cloth to cover it, made a fine sideboard for the dining-

room ; and our menu was varied by fresh vegetables
from the gardens, and by occasional presents from
the monks—compressed dates, quince-jam, and a
delicious kind of date-wine manufactured in the convent. At dinner, after sunset, we all re-assembled,
and the incidents of the day were discussed in lively
conversation. Aḥmed came in with dessert ; a handsome man, in picturesque attire, he never looked
better than on those occasions, when he stood at the
back of the tent (with the light full on his dark,
intelligent features) and began to tell us his wonderful
stories. He told of travels by land and sea, of the
pilgrimage to Mekka, and the battle of Tel-el-Kebir ;
fairy-tales like those in the Arabian Nights, amusing
anecdotes of priests and pashas outwitted by simple
fellaheen, and weird legends about the evil eye, in
whose power the most enlightened Muhammedans
seem firmly to believe. On moonless nights a lantern
was lit in the little square, to show us the way to our
beds, and we retired early to our rest, hearing only
seldom, as in a dream, the tinkling of the bell that
called the poor monks to their vigils.

The palimpsest contained about 300 pages, of which
a third fell to each of the transcribers. Mr. Harris
was an indefatigable copyist, and his tale of lines
outran in the end that of his competitors, while they
took upon themselves, beside their allotted task, the
important work of revision, when many a doubtful
letter and difficult reading yielded to their united
endeavours. And yet these insatiable scholars were

not content with the palimpsest alone. Daily, for
several hours, the abbot attended in the archbishop's
room, and produced his treasures from the hidden
closet, an armful at a time. Copious notes and
extracts were made, with a view to further publi-
cations. And not only the men were at work.
Mrs. Burkitt helped her husband by copying old
Arabic texts. Mrs. Lewis and Mrs. Gibson made
elaborate lists of all the Arabic and Syriac MSS. in
the convent ; they have since been published at Cambridge, and form a valuable foundation for further
research. Even I, by far the most ignorant of the
party, was allowed to handle the curious old books ;
I could not read a line of them, but I learned to distinguish different ages in parchment and paper, and to
mark how from century to century the shapes of the
alphabet vary. I helped Mrs. Gibson to count and
smooth the leaves of her Arabic volumes, and I ended
by copying, successfully, a MS. of ' Palestinian' Syriac,
though without understanding the meaning of the
words [1].

After a while the abbot, partly to please Mrs.
Lewis, partly to shorten his own hours of attendance,
proposed that these books also should be taken into
the garden, to be numbered and catalogued at our
convenience ; and henceforth, every morning, one of
the labourers employed in the yard came down with
his hod full of MSS. and emptied it in front of the

[1] See *Anecdota Oxon.* vol. i. pt. ix.

tents. It is not astonishing that, under similar treatment, so many valuable records of antiquity have been lost or mutilated ; my husband, who had been for many years librarian in Cambridge, felt a pang at his heart whenever he saw those coveted volumes tumbling from the basket.

But a better time has come for the library on Sinai. Much attention was called to the place by the reports of our journey, and the archbishop in Cairo, though indifferent to the Gospel of St. Peter, showed a most practical interest in the new discovery: he banished himself for nine months to the convent, and superintended the workmen in person. One of the old vacant rooms was thoroughly restored, and even furnished with glass to the windows ; the MSS. now are all neatly arranged according to number and size, and our palimpsest reposes under a glass lid in a beautifully carved box of Spanish mahogany, made in Cambridge and sent out by Mrs. Lewis. Every facility is given to scholars who wish to consult the collection, at stated hours, in the presence of a monk, but no book is allowed to leave the room, and the worm-eaten chests and the gardener's hod have alike become things of the past.

A better time for the library, certainly! yet for our personal comfort the laxity, or rather the absence, of all rules in 1893 was an unspeakable advantage. Slowly but steadily, letter upon letter and line upon line, by the help of sharp glasses and chemical agents, the long-lost Gospels were brought to light. There were, indeed, day by day, new doubts and new difficulties : lost pages, long gaps, unknown words, and shapeless letters. There were aching eyes also, and burning brows ; but, on the whole, the work prospered beyond expectation. And with all these hours of patient toil, there was hardly a day but had some special interest of its own. The walks in the rocky valley and the secret water-springs, the towering granite above and the well-tended gardens below, the different sets of pilgrims and the passing caravans, the economy of the convent and our friendship with the Greek monk Nicodemus, the habits of the Bedouin women, the traders with the skins of wild animals, and the beggars to be fed at the gate, all was new and wonderful in our eyes, and time was all too short to comprehend it.

Soon after our arrival some twenty or thirty Russian pilgrims came to the convent, apparently small farmers or peasant proprietors, men and women, led by the headman (Starost) from some village in the southern steppes. They were comfortably clothed, the men in fur-trimmed coats and caps, the women in heavy woollen skirts, and jackets with bright-coloured aprons, and neatly folded handkerchiefs over their heads and shoulders. They had guides and camels, and plenty of provisions and blankets and pillows for camping out in the desert ; and altogether there was about them an air of rustic prosperity, though they travelled without tents, and most of the men had made the journey on foot. They had started from their distant homes at the beginning of winter, on a pilgrimage of several months to Sinai and Palestine, probably assisted by wealthy landowners, for whom they had to offer up vicarious prayers at different shrines. Here they were most hospitably received by the monks, lodged in their guest-chambers, entertained at their table, and escorted to all the sacred sites of the neighbourhood. We went to see them at dinner in the refectory, a low vaulted hall, lighted by a large opening in the roof, with a little altar and burning candles at one end, and a wooden pulpit half-way down the side. Monks and pilgrims sat together at the rough, uncovered tables, and ate with a vigorous appetite. Large bowls of a savoury mess and huge brown loaves were pushed along the board, and a merry clatter of platters and spoons accompanied the monotonous voice of the priest in the pulpit, who read a Greek homily during the meal. After dinner the whole company, including our party, stood in groups near the altar, where one of the monks intoned a short service of praise. Then followed the 'Agape' of the Eastern Churches : a priest went round with a plate full of bread and gave us each a piece of it, a second priest brought a goblet of wine and gave us to drink, and chanting of prayers and responses went on all the while, until we were dismissed with a blessing.

The rite was very much like that of the Lord's Supper in the Reformed Churches of Germany. But it was not the sacrament of the Church on Mount Sinai. That was celebrated early in the morning with a grand mass at the high altar. The abbot would have admitted us, but we did not wish to intrude, and contented ourselves with some other services on Sunday, when incense and vestments, tapers and bell-ringing formed great part of the proceedings. The pilgrims stayed about a week at the convent, very quietly, but the day of their departure was exciting enough. Bedouin and camels had been summoned to carry them on their way to Jerusalem, and, as usual on such occasions, nearly twice the required number had assembled at the gate. Early in the morning they crowded into the yard; each man insisted on being employed, seized in the general scramble on some of the scattered boxes and packages, proclaimed with violent gesticulations that his camel was sufficiently loaded, and clamoured to set out on his journey. There was no dragoman to keep order, and the poor Russians were helpless in the hands of their numerous escort. But Nicodemus came to the rescue. His eye and his voice seemed to carry authority with them; he selected a number of camels and drivers for the caravan, and expelled the others from the premises, claiming obedience in the abbot's name, and enforcing it, when necessary, by sounding blows from his staff, which nobody dared to resent. They retired with scowling faces and muttered curses, but without further signs of resistance, and those who remained were compelled to carry their allotted amount, however loudly they might protest that a neighbour's beast was less heavily weighted. He went from one to the other, helping

here to lift a load, there to undo a knot, and by his
pleasant words and ready wit managed to restore
peace and goodwill between the pilgrims and their
guides ; but it was past midday before they were
ready to start, accompanied by one of the Russian
monks, to act as arbiter in case they should fall out

RUSSIAN PILGRIMS.

by the way. The women mounted their camels and
filed down the valley ; but the men stepped, one after
the other, upon the rocky platform at the opposite side
of the road, and, lifting their arms unto heaven, prayed
aloud for a blessing on the convent.

Two of the women had to stay behind : the one,
exhausted by previous exertions, was not well enough

to continue the journey; the other acted as nurse and chaperone, until they were both able to join a small caravan to Tor, a little seaport in the south of the peninsula. The invalid required perfect rest and such restoratives as Nicodemus prescribed and the convent afforded. But her friend walked in the gardens and came to our tents; and, as I was not occupied with literary labours, it fell to my lot to take her round the camp. She was a middle-aged woman, of splendid physique, with a broad forehead and thoughtful countenance. She was apparently of a very placid, or even stolid, temperament; nothing seemed to astonish or surprise her, though almost everything, from the Union Jack overhead to the Persian rug under foot, must have been new and strange to her. I took her to the cook's department, and showed her our English vessels and baking-tins, and our little cakes and sweetmeats just fresh from the oven. Yet her features remained immovable. But all at once a large cauliflower in the gardener's basket caught her attention. She took it in her arms and pressed it to her bosom, her face suffused with smiles and her eyes brimming over with tears. Did it remind her of a far-off garden, and of loving hands that tended it in her absence? We could not speak to each other, but our thoughts seemed to meet, and we shook hands warmly at parting. ' One touch of nature maketh the whole world kin.'

On the last Sunday before Lent the abbot and the steward came down to dine with us. We had sacri-

ficed our fattest turkey in their honour, and the old
abbot fairly shrieked with delight when that goodly
dish appeared on the board, clapping his hands and
smacking his lips until better employed with the
portion on his plate. The steward smiled pleasantly
at his superior's enjoyment, as you might smile at
a frolicsome child. He, Nicodemus, was not a regular
inmate of the place, but sent here by the archbishop
to put the affairs of the monastery into order, to be
transferred next year to another house for a similar
purpose. Born at Athens and educated for the priesthood, he had travelled in distant countries, and spoke
three or four languages with ease. He was now in
his prime, a true son of his Church and his order in
all humility and obedience, yet withal of a liberal and
tolerant mind. He would have made a mark in any
profession, and seemed somewhat out of place in this
wilderness among his simple and ignorant brethren.

It has been said that Sinai is a kind of reformatory,
where monks from other countries are sent to expiate
their offences in solitude and privation. As far as we
could see, our monks were docile, gentle, and industrious. They did not, indeed, spend many hours in
study, but they had not much time to be idle, being
of necessity their own bakers and brewers, their own
tailors and shoemakers, masons and carpenters. The
large orchards and gardens also, not only here, but
on other slopes of the mountain, give them plenty of
occupation. Towards us they were ever respectful
and kind. One old man was busy, morning after

morning, trimming and pruning the vines on the terrace below us. We stood by for some time watching with pleasure how deftly he used his scissors, when he suddenly dropped them, and ran away as fast as his old legs would carry him. We were afraid of having offended him, but he soon returned with a basket of beautiful raisins, which he presented to us as the fruit of these his own particular vines.

Nicodemus himself was hard at work ; he had to attend to repairs in the church, to new plantations of fruit-trees, and to the clearing and deepening of the channels that bring the water down from the mountain. Or he was absent for days together, arranging for the necessary supplies of flour and fuel and cloth, which the camels of the convent have to fetch from Suez or from Tor. Only seldom was he at leisure to come at dusk to the tents and share our afternoon tea. Those were pleasant half-hours for all of us, ' the feast of reason and the flow of soul,' and we often wondered what part Nicodemus would yet have to play in the Church of the East.

One evening Ahmed brought a little visitor with him to the dining-tent : Ayeed, the boy who had led Mrs. Burkitt's camel. Remembering how she enjoyed the goat's milk in the camp of Mokattab, the child had filled a large glass bottle (a flask thrown aside by some foreign traveller) with milk from his mother's goats, had stoppered it with a twisted rag, and carried it for eight hours across the desert as a free-will offering to his princess. He had only just arrived, and looked very hot and very tired, but supremely happy when Mrs. Burkitt thanked him for his thoughtfulness, and we all praised him for his pluck. I need not say that he had a good supper, and was put to bed in the most comfortable corner of the dragoman's tent. We wished him to rest for a day, but he was anxious to go in the morning; his mother might miss him, and he wanted to water his camel. Mrs. Burkitt gave him a large English shawl, which he draped at once dexterously around his slim little figure. One corner was over his head, and he looked proudly over his shoulder at the fringes that dangled at his heels as he went merrily on his way down the long valley. We mothers watched the solitary child with saddening eyes until he disappeared among the rocks. Yet he was a true son of the desert, seeing no danger in its loneliness, and happy enough that morning with a new cloak, with plenty of provisions for the journey, and with the hope of leading his beloved mistress for another glorious ten days across the desert. But that dream was not to be fulfilled. Hardly a week later Ahmed told us, with tears in his honest eyes, that little Ayeed's camel was dead, killed by the evil eye, the envious eye of some neighbour to whom the boy had related in childish glee the story of his good fortune in Sinai. We found the same belief in the bane of the evil eye among the poor women that came for bread to the convent. They carefully covered the little brown faces of their babies, lest we should injure them by coveting their beauty.

Twice every week, at noon, baskets of bread were let down from a window in the outer wall, and hungry hands were ever ready to receive them. Soon after sunrise on those well-known days, women and children came up from the surrounding valleys, and waited patiently for the time of the loaves. The children

WOMEN BEGGING OUTSIDE THE CONVENT.

played at 'hide and seek' among the rocks, and made a rush for baksheesh whenever we appeared at the gate ; but the women sat listless on the stones by the well. Their husbands were, most of them, in the service of the monks, tending their camels, watering their plantations, or escorting pilgrims to and fro in the desert. For nearly a year no rain had fallen in this district ; the wells were drying up, the herbage failed, camels and goats were moving further south, and several camps in the neighbourhood had already been deserted. The remaining families seemed to be destitute, depending for their maintenance on the bounty of the convent. We tried to talk to the women at the well, and to win their hearts by bringing them biscuits and sweets for their children, but only succeeded in making a couple of them into most impudent beggars. They followed us up and down the road, took hold of our clothes and put their hands in our pockets to see what we had brought for them ; a piece of sugar, a crust of bread, a bit of string, or an old button, nothing came amiss to them ; but their great desire, as indeed that of every Bedouin, was for shawls and handkerchiefs. These make turbans and belts for the men, cloaks and veils for the women, and form the whole wardrobe of their infants. We gave away all we could spare, and were sorry that we had not brought an extra supply of them.

Not knowing how much I would have to see and to do in the desert, I had brought with me a quantity of scarlet wool and knitting - needles, and I now proposed to teach one of the women to knit, that she might herself make a shawl for her baby, but my attempt was a failure. I could not understand her language ; I could not even watch the expression of her face, covered as it was, in Towara fashion, by strings of coins stretched from one ear to the other; and her hands were so grimy that I had to begin

I

my lessons by giving her a cake of soap, and by
instructing her how to employ it.   I was vexed next
day to find her little child sucking the soap, and to
see no trace of its legitimate use.   However, as the
bright colour of the wool fascinated her eyes, we
might have succeeded in spite of these drawbacks,
but for the men and boys who collected around us
whenever they saw us at work.   As soon as they
approached, the woman muffled her face in her cloak,
and there was an end of the lesson.   But the men
themselves were eager to learn, their fingers were
cleaner and quicker, and henceforth I sat many a time
in a shady corner under the wall with a tall, dark
pupil beside me, and with a little crowd of spectators
pressing unpleasantly nigh, until I drew a semicircle
in the sand with the point of my sunshade and made
them retire beyond it, not without the assistance of
sundry cuffs from my privileged neighbour.   I do not
know how long this amusement might have lasted
had not the wool been exhausted.   I divided the rest
among the most apt of my pupils, and promised to
send them a larger supply on returning to England.

We had not expected to find here so many links
with the civilized world, and were quite surprised one
morning when the steward asked us if we had any
letters to post.   A convoy of camels was going down
to Tor, where coasting vessels from Suez call now and
then for supplies.   Our pens were quickly at work,
and a goodly number of letters was given to one of
the drivers, together with money sufficient to frank

them at the little office in Tor. We heard afterwards that they all reached their destinations without undue delay, and were fully prepaid by our amateur postman. Meanwhile our letters, which had accumulated at the post-office in Suez, were forwarded to us by another caravan that escorted a party of German sportsmen to the hunting-grounds of Feirân and Sinai. They came by the same route that we had taken, and it was very amusing to receive the daily reports of their progress that were brought to us, in some incomprehensible way, by wanderers from the plain, and by goatherds from the mountain. Now they were watering their camels at Ghurundel, now camping by the sea, and now ascending Serbâl. Thus we heard of an accident that befell one of their Arab servants, wounding him seriously in the leg, and delaying their arrival for several days. At length they camped in the enclosure near Palmer's Hill, and their dragoman came up at once with our letters. There were joyful hearts in our tents that night; 'as cold waters to a thirsty soul, so is good news from a far country.' Next morning the injured man was brought to the convent. He had a gunshot wound above the knee, and had suffered much from loss of blood and want of surgical aid, though his employers had neglected nothing that could be done at the time. They were members of an ancient princely family in Germany, and provided most liberally for all his future wants before they left him in charge of the abbot.

We called at their camp to thank them for bringing our letters, but they were out, and on returning to our tents we found their coronetted cards on the table. So we missed each other, and they left on the following day, but we saw their dragoman again. He came to borrow a handful of flour to make a little cake for his master. He was one of our own former applicants, and, less experienced than Ahmed, he had reckoned too much on what might be bought by the way. His flour-barrel was empty, and his party had fallen back for several days on the coarse black loaves of the monks or the unleavened cakes of the Arabs. Meanwhile the sick man was lying on some matting under an open shed in our yard. The monks would have gladly given him one of their cells, but he could not endure the confinement of their narrow walls : and probably the free air of the mountain helped his speedy recovery. He had his own fire, his pipe, and his coffee-pot. Nicodemus acted as surgeon. a superannuated camel-driver as nurse, and our cook provided beef-tea and jellies—fortunately in double quantities, for the attendant enjoyed them as much as the patient. They got on capitally together, and both regretted the day when they were dismissed from this primitive hospital.

Our next visitor was the old sheikh from Feirân. We had never thought of seeing him again ; but there he was, with his camel at the gate, in his amplest cloak and his brightest turban, and with two miserable chickens under his arm. He had promised to restore our property; so he had captured these fowls, had carried them alive forty miles across the desert, and now delivered them to us in the presence of the abbot, that his own righteousness might be apparent to all. But he had also promised to punish the offenders; so he had confiscated their goods, and brought us a belt and a powder-horn as presents to atone for the sins of his people. The things were very old, and curiously wrought of beaten brass, inlaid with glass beads in beautiful patterns. They would have graced any museum, and we were sorely tempted to keep them, but Nicodemus advised us to send them back to their owners. The Bedouin, so he told us, value such heirlooms most highly, and as we had to cross the desert again, they would certainly try to recover them by fair means or foul, more likely the latter. So all their misdeeds were freely forgiven; the sheikh, after being well entertained at the convent, returned rejoicing to his tents, and our much-tried chickens rejoined their companions in the orchard, and lived in comfort and plenty to the end of their days.

From the first we had planned to stay a month on Mount Sinai, then to go slowly northward and to spend Easter in Jerusalem. But as week after week passed by, our students saw that they could not finish their work in time; another fortnight at least would be wanted, and they had all to resume their regular duties in Cambridge at the beginning of next term. So we had now to decide: either 'leave the present task incomplete,' or 'give up our visit to the Holy Land.' We were all assembled in council, and, whatever our secret longings for Jerusalem, we were brave enough to vote as one man for the work on Sinai. Ahmed, indeed, objected that his provisions were not calculated for so prolonged a stay; but the monks were ready to help, and we sent a couple of men with a camel to Suez (200 miles to the nearest grocer's shop) to buy what else we required. They would also, we hoped, bring us another batch of letters, and as the time approached for that camel's return, our daily walk was down to the plain, where we strained our eyes after every dark speck that appeared on the sand in the distance. Now it was a solitary monk coming home from an outlying plantation; now a Bedouin woman collecting her goats for the night; now a messenger from Feirân on his swift-trotting camel; or a whole household moving from camp to camp, mother and child sitting high above tent-poles and furniture, and the patriarchal husband striding along by the side.

Thus we watched one evening a file of camels coming across the plain towards Wady-ed-Deir. We made out the dark features and bright-coloured turbans of the drivers, but the figures of the riders remained incomprehensible: fair faces and yellow beards, with long white cloaks, and cowls tied with camel-hair string, like those of the Algerian Arabs. At length Professor Bensly went up to one of the leaders and addressed him, at a venture, in English.

The riddle was solved. This was a party of priests from the Dominican convent of St. Stephen at Jerusalem, which is a kind of training-school for Roman Catholic clergy, who come there from all parts of the world for two years at a time, to study the history of Christianity at its cradle. The young men whom we now met were on a holiday tour with their prior, and the white robes of their order were well adapted to a journey through the desert. They came from Germany, Belgium, and Scotland, and belonged to a much higher class of society than the monks on Sinai. Christian scholars and gentlemen, they showed their superior breeding by the pleasant way in which they conformed to the wishes and habits of their hosts. Though, like us, they had brought their own tents and provisions, they willingly shared the cells and the table of the convent, and joined in all its religious observances, merging the minor distinctions of Eastern and Western in the community of the Holy Catholic Church. In a similar way our Roman Catholic cook attended the convent-mass every morning ; and, strange to say, it was our Muhammedan dragoman who first obtained that permission for him by applying straight to the abbot.

After a week on Mount Sinai, the prior with his party went on towards Petra. They started early in the morning, and expected to have a hot ride across the plain, for the weather had changed with the beginning of March. When we arrived, the snow, indeed, had disappeared from the top of the mountain,

and the sun felt hot enough in the middle of the day ;
but the mornings and evenings were chilly, and once
we had so sharp a frost during the night that our
negro found a sheet of ice on his wash-tub. Amazed
at this miracle, the like of which he had never seen,
he managed to detach the transparent disk, and
carried it carefully around the camp, holding it up
before his face like a looking-glass, and calling aloud
for admiration. I am afraid he thought us very
callous; we certainly did not share his joy, but
wished for warmer weather. In our sheltered valley,
well provided with blankets and rugs, we did not
actually suffer from cold, but the mountain that
protected us from rough winds also deprived us of
sunshine. Early in the afternoon the sun dipped
below Gebel Musa, and we often went down to the
plain to enjoy its warmth, for another hour at least,
after it had set for the convent. But its power increased only too rapidly, and ere long morning and
evening had become the pleasantest part of the day.
At noon the flat rocks by the roadside felt burning
hot to the touch, and the little washstand at which
the transcribers worked throughout the day had to
be moved from place to place into the double shadow
of tents and of trees. The camel-drivers complained
of dried-up wells, the goatherds found no water for
their flocks, and the monks began to look anxiously
at the state of their reservoirs.

But on the morning of March 9, a little cloud arose
from the plain like a man's hand. Before noon the

whole heaven was black with clouds, the mist clung in white folds to the sides of the gorge, and at dinner-time the long-desired rain descended in torrents. Our servants had dug trenches outside the tents to carry off the water, and we were busy inside, covering our books and papers with waterproofs and umbrellas. But we might have saved ourselves that trouble. Though the rain continued all night, and the clattering, pattering sound on the canvas kept us awake, hardly a drop of it entered the tent, and the matting on the sandy floor was perfectly dry in the morning. After breakfast wind and rain subsided, the mist lifted like a veil from the face of the earth, and the sun reappeared in its splendour, while we remembered and realized the words of the poet: 'How the water comes down at Lodore.' Here it came roaring and pouring, and rushing and gushing, and rumbling and tumbling from the granite heights down to the wadys and wells of the desert; and here it fell from the cliffs overhead, dashing and splashing, brightening and whitening, hopping and dropping, and dancing and glancing, as it filled all the cisterns and tanks of the convent. As we walked abroad an hour later, the steep path was already dry and clean, but between the rocks on either side were deep transparent pools; and here the women washed their clothes, and the babies paddled knee-deep in the water, like English children in a summer sea. The monks were joyfully at work in their plantations, making ditches round every tree, that not a single root might miss its full share of the flood that poured in abundantly from the opened sluice-gates of the large reservoir; truly the blessing from on high that filleth all things living with plenteousness.

A new wealth of blossoms awoke in gardens and orchards, and a faint blush of spring came even to the barren desert; the ragged tufts of rumth (the rough grass that is the chief food of the camels) put forth new blades, the bedherân between the stones broke into a fragrant heather-like bloom of the palest golden-brown tint; velvety leaves, resembling our sage, peeped from the crevices in the granite; and a kind of dandelion, growing close to the ground, shone in yellow clusters at the foot of the crags. Small sand-coloured lizards sunned themselves on the top of the garden-wall, and pretty little birds (a sort of canary) fluttered from branch to branch, and picked up crumbs near the tents. A curious black swallow seemed to build its nest in the rocks above, and a flock of large black crows settled on the cypress trees or on the roofs of the convent, while now and then a vulture drew its circles high up in the sunny sky.

As the days lengthened, so also our walks became more and more extended. We had no dangers to fear; the rocks were steep, but the rough granite gave a secure foothold, and huge boulders, tossed one upon the other, formed in many places a practicable stairway. The natives whom we met in our rambles seemed to know and respect us as guests

of the convent; the women and children were inveterate beggars, but the men passed by in stately
dignity, with the usual salutation of ' Blessed be thy
day,' except once or twice, when one of my pupils,
who knitted as he walked along the plain, asked me
politely to pick up a fallen stitch. The howling of
a jackal was now and then heard in the night, but
all that we saw of wild beasts in the mountains was
a couple of panther and hyena skins, offered for sale
by a wandering Bedouin.

One of our favourite expeditions was to reach
a solitary cypress that grew on the opposite side
of the valley, about 400 feet above the path, on what
seemed from below a narrow ledge of a bare and
precipitous wall. But there were mounds of fallen
stones at the base, larger and smaller blocks of
granite higher up, vertical clefts with broken sides,
little hollow watercourses between cliff and cliff, and
projections and cavities in the rock itself, to help in
the ascent, that, after all, required more ingenuity
than strength; and from different sides and in different
ways, climbing and creeping, turning and twisting,
going up and down and from right to left, in search
of an easier stepping-stone or a safer slope, we accomplished the feat again and again. The cypress stood
on a kind of natural balcony, where the spring that
trickled from the rock at the back had hollowed for
itself a regular basin, and here a matted bed of reeds
had grown up around the roots of the tree. On a
lower platform just in front of it, some rough boulders

formed a semicircular seat, and a row of five upright stones at the edge of the cliff looked hardly like the handiwork of nature ; we saw no other trace of human habitation, but probably this was the site of some sanctuary in early Christian, or even in ante-Christian, times.

THE CONVENT, FROM ABOVE.

We had from this height a beautiful bird's-eye view of the convent. Seen from here, the massive rampart that surrounds the monastic buildings, and the lower, yet hardly less substantial, stone fence that encloses the cultivated ground, seemed like the strong sea-wall that secures some fruitful island from the inroads of the ocean. Within were the crowded roofs

with tower and dome, the intricate passages and
galleries with the humble habitations of the monks, and
luxurious masses of foliage and flower that completely
hid our little tents beneath their summer splendour.
Without was nothing but rock and sand, no sign of
life or vegetation, no trace of the hand of man. To
the left the gorge grew narrower and wilder as it rose
to the top of the pass; on the right it wound slowly
down to the plain of Er-Rakkeh, that shimmered white
in the distance. About an hour's walk from the
convent took us some way across that sunny ground
to one of the several wells that are here assigned
to the rod of Moses. It came from a narrow rift
in the granite under a sheltering cliff, and a young
acacia made a cool bower above the little rocky pool
full of mosses and water-weeds. We caught the tiny
rill in our hands as it fell from the rock above, and
we followed it on its course over the large boulders,
that formed the stepping-stones to this fountain in
the wilderness, until it was swallowed up by the
thirsty sands below.

In a neighbouring valley, on a plateau surrounded
by a theatre of picturesque rocks, we came upon the
lately deserted camp of a numerous tribe. At first
sight it looked like a burnt-out village; little en-
closures or roofless huts of loose stones, carefully
piled together, are here used instead of tents, which
would be difficult to pitch on this rocky and uneven
ground, and these primitive walls had been well
scorched and blackened by the continual fires, while

heaps of cinders and refuse were still lying in secluded corners where wind and rain had not been able to dislodge them. We saw only a few small holes, half full of muddy water, but there must have been a good supply of it at some earlier time. The traces of camels and goats were abundant, almond and olive trees had sprung up in wild disorder, and a beautiful palm stood as lonely mourner above the desolate camp. A few miles further was a rosy plantation of fruit-trees, belonging to the monks, with its well and water-tanks, and with a little house for temporary shelter, the whole secured and isolated by the usual stone fence from the barren desert without.

Another pleasant walk was past Palmer's Hill, where we got a pretty view of the convent with its flowering gardens in front, set like a picture in the narrow window frame of the little hut ; and then along Wady-es-Sheikh, to watch the graceful capers of the black goats up and down the steep cliffs, as they searched for the precious herbage which the recent rains had made to spring from the crevices. Their guardian angel, in the shape of a little maiden in dark blue draperies, sat motionless on the top of a rock ; but at eventide she descended, as nimbly as one of her kids, and in silent grace led the way down the long valley, followed by her lively flock that scampered merrily after her, though loth to leave their playground on the mountain side for the fences and fires of the camp that guarded them at night from four-footed and two-footed marauders. Now and then one of the little creatures would linger behind, until it suddenly bounded in flying leaps from the very height of the mountain, and ran in ridiculous haste to rejoin its companions, just as they disappeared in the distance. I need not say that the girl varied the monotony of her life by coming down from her throne and clamouring for baksheesh, whenever she caught sight of the travellers from the convent.

The best view of our valley we obtained from the top of Gebel Monega, a cone-shaped hill of greenish porphyry, that stands like a watch tower at the very head of the gorge. Seen from here, it stretches in one straight line down to Er-Rakkeh. The steep rocks on either side are never less than 1,000 feet high, and their rugged slopes seem to meet in the middle, only the narrowest possible bridle path leading down to the plain. The convent stands about half-way down, the gardens are hidden from sight, and the massive walls, though utterly dwarfed by the mountains around, seem but to add to the general wildness by barring the only available pass. On the other side, Gebel Monega looks down the wide valley Tarfa to far-off green pastures by the southern sea. Our longest and most interesting excursion, the ascent of the great mountain itself, was deferred to the last week, when we, dwellers in the flattest and sandiest county of England, had become duly familiar with the dizzy heights, precipitous cliffs, and rough, stony footpaths of our temporary home.

CHAPTER VI

THE MOUNTAIN

SINAI, or Horeb, is the ancient name of this mighty mountain, that rises in one broad mass from the very foundations of the earth, but lifts three separate heads unto heaven. This group, consisting of Ras-es-Safsafa (the Head of the Willow-tree), Gebel Musa, and Gebel Catarina, though it belongs to the same primary formation, is in itself quite distinct from Mount Serbâl, that stands at a distance of two days' journey, near the fertile oasis of Feirân, though the same appellation of Sinai' is sometimes given to this whole province of granite that stretches over thirty miles from north to south, to distinguish it from the limestone plateau of the Tih, and from the sandy flats of Arabia. Serbâl is the most prominent single mountain of the peninsula : its proud serrated head is seen from all points of the compass, and many learned treatises have been written on the question, whether Serbâl or Gebel Musa be the Sinai of the Bible. If Feirân, the city of the Amalekites, as it was still called in the early years of the Christian era, is identical with Rephidim, then Serbâl can hardly be

the mountain of the Law, for the oasis lies so close
at its feet that the people of Israel need not have
'departed from Rephidim to camp before the mount'
(Exod. xix. 2). Also, Serbâl does not rise immediately or abruptly from the plain; much difficult and
even dangerous ground has to be surmounted before
the traveller faces the real ascent, and the injunction
of Moses, not to draw near the mountain nor to touch
the border of it (Exod. xix. 12), would here have been
superfluous.

On the other hand, though the plain of Er-Rakkeh
is wide enough for the largest encampment, and its
mountain seems to grow straight up from the ground,
like a gigantic pulpit, the whole district looks to-day
so dry and desolate that a wise leader like Moses
would hesitate to choose it as a resting-place for his
people and his flocks. And yet there are many
springs among the rocks, and the orchards on different
slopes of the mountain do not seem to suffer from
drought. The seasons also vary, even now, very much
as to the amount of their rainfall. Two or three
successive storms, like the one we witnessed, would
fill for a time all the watercourses of the plain. But
whatever learned and scientific arguments may do for
the different theories, tradition has ever kept true
to this three-headed mountain of Sinai, and we
certainly were not inclined to doubt its authority.
According to this, Mount Safsafa, which faces the
plain, is the place whence Moses spoke to the people,
with his face shining from the presence of God, as he

K

descended from the somewhat higher top of Gebel
Musa, that rises immediately behind the convent,
half hidden by its two companions from the popular
gaze. Only from the highest point of our valley
could we see the summit of that holy mountain with
its little chapel, that is pointed out as the very

RAS-ES-SAFSAFA AT SUNSET.

spot where Moses received the Law, and is visited
by worshippers and sightseers from all parts of the
world. Gebel Catarina, the highest of the three,
stands a little to the west, and bears the name of the
saint whose body the angels are said to have buried
here after her martyrdom at Alexandria. It is in
fact separated from the mass that makes up Gebel
Musa and Gebel Safsafa by a deep gorge. On the

south side, towards Wady Tarfa, the mountain is
not quite so steep, and there Abbas Pasha ordered
a carriage road to be constructed, that he might
comfortably drive to the top. Rocks were blasted,
boulders removed, holes filled up, and the wide sweeps
of the projected road can be followed to and fro along
the lower slopes, but the death of the Sultan put
a sudden stop to it ; and the sharp stones that still
cover all the cuttings are so painful to the feet of
camels and men that so far the work is of no practical
value, and 'the Steps of the Pilgrims,' that are mentioned already in the time of the Empress Helena,
remain to this day the usual path to the top of
the holy mountain. A little wicket in the upper
boundary wall of the gardens brought us straight to
the foot of the rocks near one of the deep vertical
clefts that form a peculiar feature of the Sinaitic
range, and here we soon found the first of the 3,000
steps that lead for as many feet almost straight up to
the summit. The ancient monks or pilgrims who
thus cut their way to the height made the very best
use of every possible foothold or vantage ground, of
every natural crevice or projection, and the steps, in
consequence, are most irregular in shape and size,
intermitted now and then, when a rain-water channel
or shelving ridge offers a different mode of ascent,
and lost altogether in some sheltered hollow or level
breathing-place. But no guide is required to find
them again, going higher and higher along the face
of the cliff ; and formidably steep as they look from

below, they are tiring indeed, but not dangerous. Here are no loose, rolling stones, no slippery, treacherous inclines ; the granite of Sinai is firm and true, like its Law, that abideth for ever.

For the first half-hour we went up one side of the above-mentioned cleft, so steeply that we looked down on the pavement of the narrow courts below, until, turning a corner of the cliff, we lost convent and valley from sight, and were surrounded on all sides by the towering granite. No rain or snow had worn away the edges, no moss or lichen softened the outlines ; sharp and bare it glittered in the sunshine, with its long white veins of quartz and its cup-like hollows (the bubbles of a seething mass, many millenniums ago). We rested awhile near an overhanging rock, where a secret spring had formed a transparent pool fringed with the most delicate of maidenhair ferns. The large green leaves of some strange water plant were floating on the top, and we watched the slender stems curling upwards in golden-green spirals, and saw the fan-shaped roots clinging to the granite below. A rudely carved inscription in praise of Allah, the Most Merciful, showed that other pilgrims had lingered here and enjoyed the cool fragrance of this hidden aquarium.

A few hundred steps more brought us to the little Chapel of the Virgin. It is built of rough-hewn blocks, and looks like a piece of the rock against which it leans, except for the whitewash on roof and window-sill. The monks hold a service here once

a month ; they had also lately effected some repairs,
and their ladders and other implements that were still
lying about gave a less forsaken look to the solitary
sanctuary. Some chroniclers affirm this to be the
site of the original monastery for whose sake Justinian
built the fortress lower down. Others tell us that
the monks of St. Catarina were at one time so pes-
tered by fleas that they emigrated in a body to seek
for a cleaner abode. But here they were met by
the Virgin, who ordered them to return to their
shrines, and promised to rid them of their enemies ;
and, indeed, they vanished at the very same hour !
But travellers who have lately slept in the convent maintain it is time for such a miracle to be
repeated.

Just opposite to the door of the chapel our steps
began anew, as steep as ever, and ere long they passed
under a narrow arch between two perpendicular rocks.
Formerly a priest used to sit here, and all who went
up the mountain made their confessions to him and
received absolution. The same ceremony was repeated under a similar arch higher up, and only thus
doubly shriven were the pilgrims allowed to proceed
on their-way and to attend the solemn mass on the
summit. The tall green head of a cypress that seemed
suddenly to look down on us, peeping over the edge
of a gigantic cliff, was a strange surprise in this barren
wilderness, and made us climb upward with additional
zeal.

About 2,000 feet above the convent lies a wide,

shallow basin, surrounded on three sides by towering heights, but open towards the sunny south, and here we had the first free view over the mountains and valleys below us, as we emerged from the network of narrow gorges and deep ravines through which we had hitherto ascended. It was a warm, quiet morning, no movement in the air, no murmuring brook, no sound of bird or beast—a primaeval silence indeed to listen for the still, small voice. The chapel, dedicated from ancient times to the prophet Elijah, who is said to have dwelt in the cave underneath, stands in the midst of the hollow, and is of the simplest construction, built of the granite around it. In the little enclosure in front grow a few stunted herbs and the magnificent cypress whose roots must have found a hidden spring deep down in the clefts of the rock to maintain the evergreen crown in its solitary beauty. The chapel is opened only once a month, and we had regretted that we could not time our visit accordingly, but I doubt whether any voices of priests and choirs could have been more impressive that this holy all-encompassing silence and solitude. The engineers of Abbas Pasha had nearly reached the chapel, when they were stopped, fortunately, before disturbing the precincts of the prophet.

We had to climb another 1,000 feet higher on rough-hewn stairs, cut in the solid rock as before, but we were no longer hemmed in by cavernous cliffs; we now ascended the sacred summit itself, and the prospect widened with every step. There, on the open

mountain-side, patches of snow still whitened the
shady corners, and a transparent crust covered the
brooklet by the side of the path ; but, nevertheless,
it tripped merrily downstairs, unimpeded by its icy
canopy. At length, instead of the eternal granite,
rough masses of masonry appeared overhead ; only
five minutes more, and we landed on a little platform,
on the very top of Gebel Musa. The chapel and
the mosque that stand side by side on the edge of
the precipice are substantially built and carefully
whitewashed, but without any further attempt at
ornamentation. A little altar with the cross above,
and the kibla with a few Arabic texts, distinguish
them sufficiently from each other, and no human
art or skill could enhance the sanctity and beauty
of the place. Yet a fallen column and some old
foundations show that a church of larger dimensions
stood here in days gone by. We sat down at once
on these ancient remains, and began eagerly to eat
our kamar-ed-deen (the dry apricot-jam of the
Bedouins). Do not think that we were insensible
to the spiritual charms of the mountain, but climbing
it had been an arduous task, and for the moment
food and rest were our chief desire.

The view from this point, 8,000 feet above the sea,
takes in the whole of the peninsula, except to the
west, where Gebel Catarina, separated from Gebel
Musa only by a narrow ravine, rises yet 300 or
400 feet higher, and shuts out the Gulf of Suez and
the caravan route by Ghurundel. But Gebel Catarina

itself, with its riven sides and its buttresses of darkest granite, is a sight not easily forgotten. Towards the north, the broad bluff of Ras-es-Safsafa, though considerably lower, hides the wide plain of Er-Rakkeh, but the sandstone region beyond, and the desert of the wanderings (the limestone plateau of the Tîh) are clearly discerned in the distance. Mount Safsafa takes its name from the sacred willow that grows near a spring on its western slope. The Bedouin believe it to be the very tree from which Moses cut his miraculous rod. The valley of the monastery lies too near the base of the steep ascent to be seen from above, but the valley Es-Sheikh and the long valley of Tarfa can be easily traced in the wonderful labyrinth of Gebel and Wady that stretches south and east, far away, to where the green pastures beyond Tor and the blue sea of Akaba bound the horizon. At this height the little nooks where orchards and gardens flourish are entirely lost in the gigantic wilderness of stone; nothing meets the eye but naked rocks and barren gullies, and yet the granite varies so much in colour, according to its principal components, from black and darkest red and green down to a soft rose-tint or silvery grey, and the sunlit summits and deep narrow clefts add so many changes of light and shade, that the whole becomes a picture of indescribable beauty.

We sat long in silence on the summit of Sinai. A thunderstorm here would be awful indeed. But to-day the wind was hushed and the sky transparently

blue. Far below us three large black crows floated
in the sunny air, as if to remind us that life was not
quite extinct in the earth. We had travelled so far,
we had looked forward so long to this ascent of the
mountain, and now the achievement seemed like
unto a dream, a dream from which we did not wish
to be wakened. The air was so balmy, and the
sunshine so genial, the view so unspeakably grand,
' Nearer, my God, to Thee, nearer to Thee,' was the
involuntary cry of the soul. And yet we had to go
down. Alas, for the prose of life! We had to go
downstairs to dinner! for here we had nothing to
drink, and we must needs reach the tents before
nightfall.

Generally going down is easier than going up, but
in this case we found it otherwise. Partly because
we had now to face the steep precipices below us,
partly because we were not so fresh as in the morning,
we certainly proceeded slower and more cautiously
than before. It seemed often difficult to find a safe
place for the foot in descending, and at times we
preferred to sit down and to slide slowly and gently
from step to step, like little children on their nursery
stairs. The afternoon sun shone full on the whitened
roofs of the convent when we came out, once more,
from the intricate clefts of the mountains into our
own familiar valley, though as yet many hundred
feet above tree-tops and tents. Another half-hour's
careful climbing, and we stood again, safe and sound,
at the foot of the rocks whence we had started, well

shod, in the morning.   Now our boots were in a
deplorable state, for so sharp is the granite on those
primitive paths that it literally cut the leather into
pieces, and the soles were left, bit by bit, on 'the Steps
of the Pilgrims.'

CHAPTER VII

HOMEWARD BOUND

MARCH 20 was fixed for our departure. Unfortunately, in 1893, this was the first day of Ramadan, the Muhammedan Lent. As this always begins with a new moon, it is movable, like our Easter-tide ; but instead of only shifting from March into April, it moves slowly, with every thirteenth moon, through all the seasons of the year, and the exact date of its annual recurrence is not easy to remember. We had not taken it into consideration when making our plans. During this month of fasting the true believers are commanded to abstain from food and drink as long as they can distinguish a black thread from a white one, i. e. from sunrise to sunset. When at home, they make up for it by feasting at night, taking all possible rest in the day ; but on a journey this becomes inconvenient. Our dragoman, indeed, availed himself of a clause in the Koran, which absolves travellers for the days actually spent on the road, provided they prolong their fast into the following month, and feed, moreover, six beggars on each of the days thus transposed. Some of the drivers

followed Aḥmed's example; but others, too true to
the letter of the law, or, more probably, too poor to
comply with the feeding of beggars, bore bravely the
heat and dust of the day without taking any refreshment, not even a whiff from their pipes. All the
more were they ready to eat on the 19th, when they
brought their camels up to the convent, to camp near
the well as before.

My old friends, Ahlan and Ibrahim, were almost
the first to arrive; my husband and Mr. Burkitt also
soon recognized their old camels and drivers among
the assembly. Poor little Ayeed was absent; without
a camel, he was no longer of any use in the caravan.
This time we not only gave them a sheep to prepare
for themselves; our cook was busy all day, seething
large pieces of goat's flesh in his cauldron. Women
and children had come up in larger numbers than
usual, and bread and meat, with biscuits and oranges,
were liberally distributed amongst them. The children were especially delighted with the odds and
ends usually thrown away in a household removal;
empty match-boxes and battered mustard-tins, old
envelopes and broken pens, all made acceptable toys
for these youngsters; and they held a high carnival
on the rocks outside.

Our own last dinner in the garden inside was less
successful. Aḥmed, always intent on varying our
meals to the best of his power, had, some time ago,
purchased a kid from a passing tribe, and not finding
it fat enough for his purpose, had taken the mother

into the bargain. She was tethered in a corner, out of the way, where she found plenty of succulent food, while the little one had the free run of the camp. It was perfectly black, playful as a kitten, and soon became a general favourite. It frisked in and out of the tents, ate from our hands, and sniffed at our pockets; we quite forgot the purpose for which it had been bought, and never stopped to think yon playful kid must die.' Busy this day with packing and photographing, we had hardly missed our little pet; and it was a painful shock at dinner-time, when Aḥmed himself triumphantly bore it into the tent, dished with tomatos and covered with gravy. Out of regard for the dragoman's feelings, one or two of the gentlemen took a little piece on their plate; but we all turned away from the sight, and it did much to deepen the natural depression that is connected with every parting in this troublesome world. Early next morning our tents were struck, our water-casks filled, our chickens recaptured and caged, and before noon the baggage-train moved slowly towards the plain to prepare a new camp for us in Wady-es-Sheikh.

Meanwhile Professor Bensly and his two coadjutors were still quietly at work; the tents removed, they repaired to the well; tables and chairs folded up, they sat on a tree-trunk with the book on their knees; inkstand and blotting-books gone, they took to their pencils—every minute was precious. The book of the Gospels had not only had the writing washed out

by its ancient possessors ; it had been entirely taken
to pieces. When at last bound together, once more
to form the receptacle of his new martyrology, some
of the leaves had been lost, other parchments had
got mixed with the rest, half of them were turned
upside down, and hardly two sheets remained in their
consecutive order. The identification of the separate
pages formed no small part of our work, but great
progress had been made during the last fortnight ;
and it had been delightful to watch how verses and
sentences, recovered from different parts of the volume,
came together, crystallized, as it were, into chapters
and paragraphs. Now, *nearly* the whole of the 300
pages was copied, *nearly* each of the doubtful variations was doubly revised, *nearly* all the wonderful
work was accomplished—*nearly*. Oh ! for a few more
days to give it the finishing touch !

But time was up. The University of Cambridge
recalled her professor ; the steamer at Alexandria
would not delay ; the camels, once summoned to the
convent, could not be kept without fodder ; and we
had to go to the room of the abbot to bid him 'good-
bye.' For the first time we found him in his ampler
robes, with the heavy gold chain and jewelled cross
that are the badge of his office. Maybe that the
quiet presence of the great English professor, for
whom he had shown, all along, a dumb kind of rever-
ence, had unconsciously influenced his manner and
mien ; he certainly made a better figure to-day than
when he received us some six weeks ago. His table

was covered with charters and plans and other
ancient relics of the convent, and in the middle stood
a silver dish, full of transparent gold-coloured grain,
the manna of the Bible (as the monks believe it to
be). It is the resin that oozes and drops from the
tarfa-tree, a dwarfed kind of terebinth, during the
hottest months of the year. The Bedouin spread
their cloaks on the ground and collect the sweet
grains in the morning. They taste, indeed, like
wafers made with honey, but have in addition a
decidedly turpentine flavour. We were all presented
with tiny boxes of manna ; and though, in the course
of a year or two, it has shaken down and melted into
a wax-like compound, its taste remains unaltered to
this day. The abbot next opened the visitors' book,
and we looked at the list of distinguished travellers
who, from times immemorial, have visited this place.
Probably there exists no other volume of the kind
that has among its entries so large a proportion of
well-known and illustrious names. I was timid about
adding my own to so royal a register, but I found
that I had the distinction of being the first German
woman whose signature appears in this book. May
I have many successors !

We had signed our names, returned our books,
and made the usual donations to the chest of the
convent. The abbot had given to each of us a small
golden ring with the monogram of St. Catarina, in
memory of our visit to her shrine, and we had taken
a solemn farewell of each other in Greek and in

English. The riding camels had been sent forward
to Palmer's Hill, and we were to follow on foot, but
went first quietly to take leave of the garden, of
our snug little home in the desert. We found it
occupied by strangers. A party of American travellers, a father with two Nimrod-like sons, had
arrived and pitched their tents while we were engaged
with the abbot: a new dragoman and cook were
installed by the well, a new dining tent occupied the
centre of the ground, a new flag, with stars and stripes,
was hoisted instead of the Union Jack, and already
our place knew us no more. Like the Russian pilgrims, we stopped awhile on the rocks on the other
side of the road, to take a long last look at the
convent ; and again and again, as we went slowly
down the winding path, whose every furlong was
now familiar to our feet, did we turn to catch another
glimpse of those white roofs and blossoming trees,
with the towering granite behind them. The day had
been one of the hottest, and had made us dread the
coming ten days in the desert ; but as we emerged
from the narrow valley a fresh breeze met us, blowing from the north across the plain of Er-Rakkeh. We
did not now cross it, but turned to the right, eastward,
and walked, through the pleasant evening hours, by
the side of our camels, down the wide valley Es-
Sheikh, until the sun set behind us, and the camp
fires gleamed in the distance—not only our own
this time ; a large Bedouin tribe, migrating from
winter to summer pastures, was resting in a bend of

the valley; and their singing and shouting, together with the barking of their dogs and the growling of their camels, resounded far into the night, for they had kept the first day of Ramadan, and were now released, by the darkening sky, from their fasting. Henceforth Aḥmed had a special gong sounded at

LEAVING THE CONVENT BY THE WADY-ES-SHEIKH.

the precise moments of sunrise and sunset, to remind our followers of their religious duties.

The wind remained in the north the next fortnight, and though at times disagreeable enough to fill our eyes with sand and to blister our faces, it tempered the noon-day heat to such a degree that we felt it less oppressive now at the end of March than during our journey in January. Moreover, the clouds, whose

L

blessing we witnessed in the mountain, had swooped down on the lowlands also with healing in their wings ; and though the watercourses seemed now as dry as ever, the effects of a recent passage of waters were apparent on every side—in the fresher blades of the rumth, in the stronger scent of the bedherân, and even in tiny flowerets, like diminutive daisies, that just peeped here and there from the sun-baked soil, as if afraid of lifting their pale golden eyes above the sandy surface.   Repeatedly we rested among groups of tarfa-trees, pleasantly green to the eyes, though the brittle branches showed no sign of the sweet resin that exudes from them later in the year ; the juniper bushes that studded some of the lower reaches were covered with white flower-spikes, and would not have looked amiss in an English shrubbery; and altogether this side of the mountain seemed less barren and desolate than the way by which we had come up.   The days were longer now, yet we rose with the sun as before ; we had a good rest in the middle of the day, and 'nightly pitched our wandering tents a day's march nearer home.'   The summit of Sinai was hidden, only too soon, by intervening heights, but Serbâl reappeared in its glory. Black, purple, or blue, according to the distance or the time of the day, it seemed to accompany us, like a faithful friend, during the greater part of the week. We exchanged the dark massive cones of granite for the many-clefted and many-coloured sandstone, whose fantastical shapes our imagination construed into temple-gates and gigantic sphinxes; and our camels made wide detours whilst we scrambled over rocky ridges or down steep inclines into some lower valley, until the hills became rounder and the watercourses shallower, and we struck once more into Wady Shebêkah, to return by our former route via Ghurundel to Suez. Our buried bottles were easily recovered, and their sparkling contents proved a great comfort during our last three days in the desert, which managed, somehow, to be the most trying of all the campaign.

We spent a quiet Sunday among the palms of Ghurundel, under a grey and hazy sky, a very unusual sight in that district. The wind had gone down, the broad green fans of the dom-palm had forgotten their waving, the camels seemed to sleep through the live-long day, and a drowsy silence brooded over the camp. The natives prophesied a storm, but though a few heavy drops fell in the afternoon, and the men began to dig rain-trenches about the tents, no disturbance occurred during the night.

Next morning the wind blew hard from the north, but still the sun was hidden by that strange haze, that seemed to deepen as we rode on. A Turkish officer and his orderly joined our cavalcade; they were on duty, bound from Tor to Suez, and though mounted on swift-trotting camels, preferred to ride slowly by our side, for the sake of the greater security which larger numbers afford. A stray dog had also a few days before, attached itself to our company

Nobody knew whence it came; it was seen, in the heat of the day, limping painfully by the side of the camels, and snapping up greedily a morsel of bread that somebody threw to it. At the next halt we gave it some water, and in the evening it was regaled with chicken-bones, and found a place by the kitchen fire. Henceforth it became an inseparable member of the caravan, and changed so much in appearance, that its owners (if indeed it ever had an owner) would not have known it again. Emaciated, mangy, and wolfish-looking, when we first made its acquaintance, it soon got sleek, well-conditioned and frolicsome, never tired of wagging its tail or of licking the hands of its benefactors.

But to-day even the dog partook of the general depression. At midday a tent was summoned from the rear to protect us from the wind and from the flying grit that threatened to mix with our food. So we lunched under canvas, and when, on resuming our ride, we discovered, from the top of a sand ridge, first the long range of the African mountains, and then a shining belt of dark blue sea, we forgot all present discomforts and hailed the beautiful sight with loud exclamations of joy, like the 'Thalassa, Thalassa!' of old. But soon everything in front of us was obscured by a dark yellowish cloud. Did it advance towards us, or did we ride bodily into it? I do not know. Suddenly the sand-storm was upon us. Like sharp needles it stung our faces, but only for a moment; my camel wheeled instantly round and stood perfectly still, its legs wide apart and its long neck hanging down to the ground, while the storm raged on from behind. Other camels were made to lie down, and rider and driver found some shelter to leeward, but my Ibrahim managed to be absent, my eyes were perfectly blinded with dust, and I could not dismount without assistance. So I drew my cloak over my face, bowed low on my pommel, and tried to emulate my camel in patience. Hardly ten minutes, and the storm had swept by. Fortunately it was only the hem of its garment that had thus over-shadowed us. The thick cloud passed away to the south, but the air was still full of fine particles of sands that shone like so much silver in the rays of the sun. Seen through this medium the nearest objects looked like gigantic spectres moving in the distance. Slowly the atmosphere cleared, and camels and men resumed their normal proportions ; my husband had indeed been close to me all the time, though hidden for awhile, as it were, in the valley of the shadow of death. How happy to find him again, face to face, in the full perfection of daylight !

Our guides, bewildered by the storm, had become uncertain as to the direction of the baggage-train, and wandered from right to left for the next hour or two, in vain endeavours to find a trace of their comrades. At length some landmark on the horizon gave us a clue, and led us, though later than usual, in safety to our camp in Wady Sadur. The wind was still high ; there had been some trouble in setting up the tents, and the men were busily shovelling and piling up sand to keep the curtains down to the ground. We had to go to bed without candles ; at midnight the canvas just over my head was nearly torn away by a sudden blast, and in a neighbouring tent the washstand collapsed with all its belongings. It took some time before order was restored in the dark ; but Aḥmed and his faithful satellites kept patrolling the camp, tightening the ropes and hammering down the tent-pegs, and we fell sound asleep again, notwithstanding our rocking poles and our flapping curtains. The following day was warm and clear, without a speck on sky or sand to mar their dazzling blue and white—a perfect day of the desert. The wind was still in our face, but it now blew softly, straight from the sea and from the mountains beyond, and the well-remembered head of Mount Ataka, the guardian of Suez, was already in sight.

Our return journey had, by contract, been divided into ten equal stages of twenty to twenty-five miles a day, and hitherto we had strictly adhered to that programme without undue fatigue for man and beast ; but lately Mrs. Lewis and Mr. Harris, intent on forwarding certain letters to Europe by an earlier mail, had inclined to forced marches ; and, finding my husband and myself unable to join them, they now decided on pushing on without us, accompanied by several attendants and by a certain number of baggage-camels, hoping to reach Suez twenty-four hours before the rest of the caravan. We readily agreed, but realized only at the moment of starting that the dragoman also was to be of their party. We did not like to interfere with his arrangements, but I confess we did not feel comfortable, camping in the desert without that paternal protector, especially as we were now in a comparatively inhabited district not far from Ayin Musa, and might experience another night-scene like that at Feirân. However, Mrs. Burkitt, as good an interpreter as Aḥmed himself, remained with us ; we trusted to her powers of persuasion, in case of any difficulty with the natives ; and though our slumbers were somewhat disturbed by dreams of shrieking fowls and felonious sheikhs, we fared, on the whole, none the worse for this desertion. In the morning, indeed, Aḥmed's absence was felt in the leisurely way of packing and saddling ; we started at nine instead of seven, and rode for the first time in company with the whole caravan ; but as there remained for us only half a day's ride to the place of embarkation, we could afford to take it easy. At eleven o'clock we reached Ayin Musa, wandered awhile among its palm-trees and water-springs, and found enough biscuit and kamar-ed-deen in our saddle-bags to make up for the dragoman's luncheon-box. Before noon we were once more under way, first straight down to the sea, then northward, along the barren desolate shore ; while the mountains, and the towns of Tufikieh and Suez, and large steamers bound for the canal, and a whole fleet of fishing-boats with huge brown sails bathed in brightest sunshine, made a beautiful panorama on

the opposite side of the gulf. We soon recognized
the little breakwater where we sat on our luggage
two months ago and waited in vain for the camels.

But to-day the wind was too strong for sailing
against it, and we had ridden several miles further,
when the welcome figure of Ahmed seemed suddenly
to rise up from the sea. He had taken his travellers
safely to the hotel at Suez, and had recrossed early
this morning to come to our assistance. As our
sheikh, with his men and camels, was to be dismissed
on this side of the Red Sea, not only we ourselves, with
our servants and other belongings, but also the proper-
ties of the dragoman—tents, furniture, cooking utensils,
and all that remained of the stores, had here to be
shipped. Six chickens were all that survived of our
poultry, and these, though much reduced by their
ten days' ride, were destined, as a valuable present,
for Ahmed's wife; fowls fattened on the holy mountains would be without peers in all Egypt! To
transfer so many goods from the camels to the large
cargo-boat, lying some way off the shore (as the water
was too shallow for her to come in), proved a tedious
affair. The boatmen, with their petticoats girt about
their loins, had to carry each separate bale on head
and shoulders for twenty or thirty yards through the
water that rose up to their waist as they staggered
with their heavy burdens to the side of the boat.
These fine, bronze-coloured men, clad above in loose
white shirts, embroidered waistcoats, and bright
turbans, while their drenched nether garments clung

close to their limbs, did not look unlike the legendary mermen of old, with their wet and slimy tails, as they rose half out of the water to receive a new load from the dragoman.

We had ample time to give a last biscuit to our camels, and a last baksheesh to our drivers, and to say 'good bye' for ever to these faithful creatures that had carried and guided us so quietly across the desert. We picked up a few more shells from Sinaitic sands; then we mounted, each of us, the shoulders of one of the aforesaid mermen, and were safely deposited on board. Our dog had watched all these proceedings with the utmost attention; he seemed much attached to us, and some of our party were inclined to acclimatize him in England. The journey, indeed, was a doubtful difficulty, but we all agreed to put the dog on his trial; if he were brave enough to swim out to the boat, he would be taken on board. We looked at the dog, and the dog looked at us; we called and whistled, he barked and whined, he put his feet in the water, but drew them back again; and suddenly he turned away from the shore and trotted contentedly inland, probably to join the flesh-pots of another caravan.

Meanwhile we set sail and tacked slowly to and fro, but the barge was heavily laden; moreover it leaked, and baling with a tin pot seemed to be the order of the day. Several times we touched the bottom, and at length, midway between Asia and Africa, we ran gently aground on a sand-bank.

Instantly half a dozen of our men were overboard, with the water up to their armpits, trying to shove us off, and the sails were strained to the utmost, that the wind might help to set us free. But soon all efforts were deemed fruitless until the turning of the tide, and a small boat was hailed to take off the passengers. More rowing than sailing we neared the shore, but within a hundred yards of the quay we stuck once more fast in the mud. This time we were hauled off by ropes, amid the cheering of an excited crowd that had collected to clamour for baksheesh.

Our table at the hotel was covered with letters and papers from England; and ere long we were once more steeped in the social and political interests of the West. It felt strange and stuffy that night to sleep between brick walls. Our little room had no window, only a glass door opening into the public yard, that had to be shut and bolted, and did not allow the fresh air of the desert to breathe on our pillows. We had hoped to rest a few days at Suez and to go up the canal, but a telegram from Alexandria warned us that the *Cathay*, in which we had taken our passage, was bound to leave on the morrow. So, packing in haste and taking a hurried farewell of our fellow-travellers and of Ahmed, my husband and myself started at two p.m. by a slow train for Benha, a station on the main line, to wait there for the night mail from Cairo. We halted at many a little station in the desert, but never long enough to get out or to obtain any kind of refreshment, until we stopped finally, several hours after sunset, at Benha, or rather at the station called by that name, some ten minutes' walk from the place itself.

The offices and waiting-rooms were closed for the night, as the mail train was not due before two in the morning, and the other passengers had quickly dispersed. A sleepy porter took possession of our luggage and deposited it under an open shed; then he put out the lights and retired to his lair, and we two were left, tired and hungry, to shift for ourselves in this unknown land. Fortunately the moon was bright, and the sound of laughter and singing reached us from the town, where the pious observers of Ramadan were keeping their nightly feast. So we wandered, hand in hand, through the balmy night air, and over the silver sand towards the coloured lamps in front of the cafés, where the men sat drinking and smoking, while the dancing-girls performed and the story-tellers spun their long yarns. We passed by some of the noisier groups and sat down in a quiet corner, where the little waiter, unsolicited, at once served us with coffee. We made him understand that we were hungry, but he only brought us another can full of coffee, and when we straightway asked him for bread, he looked at us with wandering eyes: this was neither the place nor the time for eating, yet he gave us a large, coarse lump, evidently a piece of his own private loaf, and we had a substantial meal of bread and coffee, the charge for both together being one piastre (or 2½*d.*);

but I believe the man made us pay for the coffee alone, and looked on the bread as a charitable gift to needy wayfarers.

Amused and refreshed, we retraced our steps to sit on our luggage, dozing and dreaming, and waiting for the train. At its approach the little station awoke, the lamps were lit, and beggars, porters, and hawkers of every kind appeared in vast superfluity. The train was crowded; we found but scant accommodation, and had to sit bolt upright for the rest of the night on narrow wooden benches, much less comfortable than our boxes and rugs in the little shed at Benha. The sun was rising above the wide waters of the Nile as we came to Alexandria. Before we could get out of the carriage we were surrounded and seized by clamorous cabmen, by touts, guides, and dragomans, who would not let us stir without their assistance; but we had learned something during these three months in the East. We recovered our property from their clutches, secured an *arabeeya*, and rolled quickly away to the harbour—one of the largest harbours in the world, with miles of piers, quays, and break-waters, and with the flags of all nations flying from innumerable mastheads. After much directing and misdirecting our driver found the wharf of the P. and O. Company, and a few minutes later we were installed in a comfortable cabin, and enjoyed an excellent breakfast.

As our boat was not to leave before noon, we paid another visit to the far-famed town—the creation of

Alexander the Great, the theatre of Cleopatra's con-
quests, the earliest high school of Christianity, and now
the chief emporium of our commerce with the East. It
was this latest aspect that most interested us just now;
and in the beautiful but entirely modern Place Mehemet Ali, we easily found a banker and a shoemaker to
minister to our wants—since our last mountain scramble
I had been reduced to a pair of velveteen slippers.
Punctually at twelve o'clock we threw off the ropes,
but it took several hours of starting and stopping, of
backing and turning, before we got free of the crowded
shipping and steamed past the high lighthouse on
the outer bar. And then all at once, as by magic, the
long low coast of Egypt sank below the water, and
we were alone on the blue Mediterranean. A light
breeze hardly rippled the surface, and the blue turned
to purple and rosy-red as the sun neared the horizon.
We were walking up and down the deck, but felt
more like walking on the pier of some seaside resort,
so steady was the steamer!

It was Easter Eve, and a prayer-meeting went on
in the second-class saloon on the lower deck. The
skylights were open, and leaning over the railing we
caught the sweet strains of an old English hymn, just
as the golden disk dipped beneath the waves, and
darkness overshadowed the earth. The glory of the
day had departed, but we were not left comfortless:
already the east was beginning to brighten, and
slowly the full moon mounted into the sky, silvering
each tiniest ripple, and pouring a river of jewels across

the slumbering sea.   The sun indeed had set for the
night, but his light lived on in the moonbeams, and
abode with us in our narrow cabins below, until the
day broke and the shadows fled away, and a glorious
Easter morning rose above the world.

CHAPTER VIII.

THE SINAI PALIMPSEST AND THE GREEK TEXT OF THE GOSPELS.

[Mr. F. C. Burkitt has permitted the author and publishers of this volume to reprint the following passages from a paper read by him on the 'Sinai Palimpsest' at the Church Congress in 1895.]

IN a few words the importance of the Syriac Palimpsest of the Four Gospels, lately found by Mrs. Lewis and Mrs. Gibson in the Convent of St. Catherine on Mount Sinai, consists in this. I believe the Sinai Palimpsest to be a very faithful representative of the earliest Syriac translation of the Gospels. The palimpsest itself is a vellum MS. written in the fourth or the early part of the fifth century, but the version of which it is a copy is very much more ancient. This version is certainly older than the Peshîttâ (Peshitto), which is not earlier than the fourth century; probably older than the Syriac Diatessaron, which is not earlier than 170 A.D. Of

this version of the Gospels only one other MS.
is known to survive besides our palimpsest, namely,
the Codex in the British Museum used by Cureton ;
from this, however, more than half the contents are
wanting, and its text has certainly undergone revision
from the Greek. In the Sinai Palimpsest considerably more than three-fourths of the whole of the
Gospels is legible, and its text shows no clear signs
of revision from later Greek MSS.

What, then, can we learn from this second century
translation of the Gospels, of which we now have so
excellent a representative in the Sinai Palimpsest ?
From what class of Greek MSS. has it been translated ?

A very few words upon the types of text found
in Greek MSS. of the Gospels may here be convenient. The so-called *Textus Receptus* must always
be our first standard of comparison in estimating
the value of a new MS. ; not because it chanced
to be that of the ordinary printed editions and of
our English Authorized Version, but because it really
is the text that has been generally current in the
Greek Church ever since the fifth century. This is,
in fact, the text found in the vast majority of our
thousand and more Greek MSS. of the Gospels.
With this text the Latin Vulgate and the Syriac
Vulgate (commonly called the Peshîttâ) often agree,
but it differs very greatly from the text of the
Ante-Nicene Church. It is not the text of our two
oldest Greek MSS., א and B, nor again of the Old

Latin versions and the associated Codex Bezae, generally quoted as D. For this reason it appeared to Dr. Hort that the general uniformity of the rest of our Greek MSS. of the New Testament was not a sign that they had faithfully preserved the apostolic original, but was the result of an official revision early in the fourth century. This revised edition became a kind of standard to which subsequent MSS. were conformed. It seems to have taken place at or near Antioch in Syria, so that the text embodied in it is generally called ' Syrian ' or ' Antiochian.' I shall use the term ' Antiochian,' because of the possible confusion between the ' Syrian ' Greek text and MSS. written in the Syriac language.

Now it is the simple fact that no purely ' Antiochian ' reading occurs in the Sinai Palimpsest. A marked illustration of this statement is found in its steady rejection of the 'conflate' readings, i.e., passages where two ancient rival readings have been fused together in the Antiochian text. Here is an illustration. In Mark ix. 49, אB and their few supporters read *For every one shall be salted with fire ;* instead of this Codex Bezae and the Old Latin versions have *For every sacrifice shall be salted with salt*, a reminiscence of Leviticus. The Antiochian text, on the other hand, with the Latin Vulgate, the Peshîttâ, and all the later versions, brings together the two rival readings, producing the familiar combination, *For every one shall be salted with fire, and*

M

every sacrifice shall be salted with salt. But the Sinai
Palimpsest has only *For every one shall be salted with
fire,* thus agreeing exactly with אB and, I may add,
the English Revised Version.

This is but one instance of the way in which
the new MS. supports Dr. Hort's theory of the
Antiochian revision of the Greek text of the New
Testament. The theory demanded that no Antiochian
reading should occur in the Old Syriac version; a
MS. of the Old Syriac version is found, and no
Antiochian reading occurs in it.   Never has a critical
theory been so signally confirmed by subsequent
discovery of new material.   It is a pathetic circum-
stance that the great scholar passed away but a few
months before the transcription of the MS.

The Sinai Palimpsest supports the text of Westcott
and Hort in many other respects besides the rejection
of Antiochian readings.   In particular, it is singularly
free from interpolations.   Thus the Lord's Prayer in
St. Luke consists of only five petitions, as in our
Revised Version; the episode of the Bloody Sweat
and the prayer *Father, forgive them,* are altogether
absent.   In St. Matthew the passages about 'dis-
cerning the face of the sky,' and the devils 'which
go not out save by prayer and fasting,' are not read.
The Gospel of St. Mark ends at xvi. 8, without a trace
of the 'last twelve verses;' in fact, the Gospel of
St. Luke begins on the same column with hardly
a break.   In this our MS. differs from the
Curetonian. MS., which had the twelve verses

as well as the longer form of the Lord's Prayer. But the passages absent from the Sinai Palimpsest are not all found in the Curetonian; in many cases the Curetonian agrees with the new MS. in omissions. The inconsistency of the Curetonian in this respect tends to show that the Sinai Palimpsest, which omits all these interpolations, here accurately represents the original form of the Old Syriac translation.

But the agreement of our MS. with B and Dr. Hort is not confined to the absence of interpolations. A good example is Luke iv. 44, where we read in אB and the Sinai Palimpsest, 'And He was preaching in the synagogues of *Judaea*;' instead of 'in the synagogues of *Galilee*,' as in the received text and the Latin versions. But perhaps the most remarkable instance is found in St. Mark's account of St. Peter's denial. St. Mark, alone among the four Evangelists, mentions the double cock-crow, but in as few words as possible. Accordingly we find great variety of reading in the four verses of chapter xiv. where the incident is mentioned, and the only authorities which consistently supported the text of Westcott and Hort were B, a Greek lectionary, and the Coptic. To these we can now add the Old Syriac, for in each of the four places the readings so acutely defended by Dr. Hort are found in the Sinai Palimpsest.

Coincidences so striking as these between B and the Sinai Palimpsest are all the more weighty as the two MSS. are shown by other readings to be wholly independent witnesses. Where they agree they agree in preserving the right reading; and it is a principle of textual criticism that only when MSS. agree in wrong readings we may assume any close relationship between them. Moreover, the allies of the two MSS. are geographically very different. The chief ally of B is the Coptic (also called Memphitic), i.e. the version of Lower Egypt. The Sinai Palimpsest, on the other hand, is often allied with D and the Old Latin versions—with those types of Greek text, in fact, which, whatever may have been their origin, were so widely spread in the second century, and which are generally compre-hended under the convenient but misleading name of 'Western.'

Instances of such 'Western' readings in the Sinai Palimpsest are innumerable; among the more note-worthy are the geographical variant, *Magedan* for *Dalmanutha*, in Mark viii. 10, and the striking ex-pression 'being grieved for the *deadness* of their hearts,' in Mark iii. 5, instead of *hardness*, or rather *blindness* (νεκρώσει for πωρώσει); it also has *last* for *first* in Matt. xxi. 31; a curious reading, whereby the Jews are made to answer that the son in the parable who said, 'I go, sir, and went not,' was the one who obeyed the will of his father. In John iii. 6, according to the Sinai Palimpsest, our Lord says to Nicodemus, 'That which is born of the flesh is flesh, and that which is born of the Spirit is spirit, *for God is (a) Living Spirit.'* Some people have accused our palimpsest of being a heretical copy of the Gospels. St. Ambrose, who was accustomed to read this verse much as it stands in the Sinai MS., says that the ordinary text is here heretical. He complains that the words, 'For God is Spirit,' had been cut out from this passage by the Arians. I see no reason for thinking that either charge of heresy is well founded.

In these and many similar instances the Sinai Palimpsest agrees with the Old Latin versions and with Codex Bezae (where extant), but with scarcely any other surviving Greek MS. Nevertheless it must not hastily be assumed that the Old Syriac and the Old Latin versions are fundamentally related in text. In saying this I am aware that the exact opposite is very commonly believed. At present I am only pleading for a suspension of judgement in the matter. It is in any case the misfortune of the Old Syriac version that its most characteristic peculiarities are inadequately represented in surviving primary Greek MSS. We have to make up for the deficiency by collecting the scattered readings which have escaped Antiochene revision in certain groups of cursives. One such group agrees with our MS. in inserting the name *Jesus* before *Barabbas* in Matt. xxvii. 16, 17, so that Pilate's question runs, *Whom will ye that I release unto you? Jesus Barabbas, or Jesus which is called Christ?* This remarkable reading was known to Origen, but it is by no means certain that it did not originate in a scribe's blunder.

After all, the most important single piece of evidence brought forward by the new discovery is the complete absence of the so-called 'last twelve verses' of St. Mark in the Sinai Palimpsest. It is worth noticing how the geographical chain of evidence against the twelve verses has been thereby extended. From Carthage, from Egypt, from Palestine, and now from Syria, the earliest texts are all unfavourable, while the only second century evidence for the verses comes from Italy and Gaul. Even Tatian lived in Rome.

There is one new reading which I am inclined to think has received already more attention than it deserves. This is the reading of the Sinai Palimpsest in Matt. i. 16, where the common text reads, *Jacob begat Joseph the husband of Mary, of whom was born Jesus, who is called Christ.*' Instead of this we find in our palimpsest : *Jacob begat Joseph; Joseph, to whom was betrothed Mary the Virgin, begat Jesus who is called Christ.*

Textual critics know that this reading, unique as it is, does not stand absolutely isolated; for in the 'Ferrar Group' of Greek MSS., in the Old Latin, and in the Curetonian Syriac, we read (with minor variations) as follows: *Jacob begat Joseph, to whom being betrothed Mary the Virgin brought forth Jesus Christ;* the word for 'begat' and 'brought forth' (ἐγέννησεν) being identical in the Greek.

The conflicting claims of these readings with the common text certainly present a very interesting critical problem. The common text is found in ℵB and indeed all Greek MSS. but two; it is also supported by Tertullian (*de Carne Christi,* 20). On the other hand, we have seen that some form or other of the alternative is supported by both the ancient second-century versions. When we examine these rival readings, we find that each of them contains an expression which might give offence to a casual reader. That this is the case with regard to the reading of our palimpsest is obvious; but we have evidence also that the expression 'husband of Mary' in the ordinary text proved a stumbling-block in ancient times. Moreover, each of the rival readings contains a suspicious phrase. It is easy to see how the ἐγέννησεν, 'he begat,' of the Sinai text might be paraphrased into ἐξ ἧς ἐγεννήθη, 'she from whom was born.' On the other hand, if the received reading be the result of a correction in the interest of the ordinary belief as to the birth of Christ, how are we to explain the presence of the title 'Mary the Virgin,' in the (supposed) heterodox version, and its absence in the (supposed) orthodox one?

It is not, however, critical niceties of this description which directed attention to our MS. at the moment of publication, but a feeling that if the reading of the Sinai Palimpsest be that of the authentic text of the Gospel of St. Matthew, our ideas as to the historical events of the Nativity would undergo a revolution. This feeling I believe to be altogether erroneous. No possible historical conclusion, no possible light upon the facts of the Nativity, could ever be deduced from the genealogy which the First Evangelist has placed at the head of his Gospel. Had the statement that Jesus was the son of Joseph been found in the genealogy given by St. Luke, the case would have been very different, for there is nothing directly to show that the lineage of Joseph there given does not contain the names of his actual ancestors up to David and beyond. But the genealogy in St. Matthew is too artificial to be the record of an actual line of descent; it is rather the Evangelist's statement of claim that Jesus Christ was the Heir of David. Even should we accept the reading of the Sinai Palimpsest, the statement 'Joseph begat Jesus' would mean no more than the parallel one, 'Jechonias begat Salathiel'—that Jechonias of whom Jeremiah prophesied with such tremendous emphasis (Jer. xxii. 30): *Thus saith the Lord, Write ye this man childless.*

There can be little doubt that the genealogy in St. Matthew was shaped into its present form by the Evangelist himself, not borrowed from a previously existing document. The whole question therefore is narrowed into the meaning the evangelist wished in this genealogy to attach to the word ἐγέννησεν, 'begat.' Now it is open to the critic who does not accept the virgin birth to base his rejection of it on the silence of St. Mark, St. John, and

St. Paul; but to claim that the man who compiled our Canonical Gospel of St. Matthew did not believe in the virgin birth of our Lord is absurd. The reading of the Sinai Palimpsest in the disputed passage, even if it be accepted as the authentic text of the Gospel, leaves the old difficulties exactly as they were.

OXFORD : HORACE HART
PRINTER TO THE UNIVERSITY

www.ingramcontent.com/pod-product-compliance
Ingram Content Group UK Ltd.
Pitfield, Milton Keynes, MK11 3LW, UK
UKHW042153280225
455719UK00001B/310